I0617178

THE
CONTRIBUTIONIST
~~MANIFESTO~~
Compromise

CAPITALISM WITH A SIDE OF ETHICS AND DECENCY

CARL FISK

ISBN 979-8-9925540-0-7

Book Cover by Andy Meaden

Edited by Michael Mau

Illustrations courtesy of multiple sources — see bibliography

1st edition Paperback, 2025

Contents

The Contributionist Compromise

FOREWORD

I think most readers will agree: we've got a lot of problems in our country at the moment. Left or right, times are becoming increasingly difficult and uncertain for the majority of Americans. When times get harder, people experience fear and stress. They become more prone to impatience and anger, and naturally, they begin looking for the causes of their woe.

The political parties in our country don't mind this at all — they'll gladly point the finger at whatever cause they think will get them the most votes. But here's the thing: regardless of which political party is elected, regardless of stimulus or tax breaks, our quality of life seems to keep trending downward. From our ability to purchase homes to the price of healthcare, to the cost of basic necessities, things are continuing to get harder for the vast majority of our society. So, perhaps the issues the parties promise to address are not the core of our problems.

Many of the troubles we're facing today are due to something we see repeatedly throughout history: the consolidation of wealth at the top, leaving less and less for the rest of the population. Throughout the ages, countries and civilizations have tried different approaches to address this problem. Most recently, capitalism and communism have emerged as the dominant economic systems. Both have the same problem: whether through greedy government officials or greedy corporations, each leads to corruption and exploitation.

We've tried very different approaches, but none of them appear to be working. What this tells me is that we need to think differently. As

Einstein said, "You can't solve a problem with the same mind that created it."

Humanity has proven time and again that we are excellent at going to extremes — that's easy for us. When we want to fix a system, we often go so far in a different direction that we create new problems and wind up in the same mess. Czarist Russia to the Soviet Union. Iranian monarchy to Islamic theocracy. Weimar Germany to Nazi Germany. Chugging cigarettes to chugging vapes.

Yes, we need a change. However, we must approach the problem in a different way than those who have grappled with it in the past. We must use nuance. *The Contributionist Manifesto* is my attempt at taking capitalism — a system with solid foundations — and injecting it with some ethics and morality. Despite unpleasant associations with the term "manifesto," this isn't a call to tear everything down; it's a series of small tweaks and changes that are possible to implement within our current system while preserving the benefits of capitalism.

But why should you listen to me? Who even am I? What makes me think I can contribute any insight?

My background and experiences have made me a person of opposites. I was born and raised in the small town of Phoenix, N.Y. My upbringing was conservative and Christian, but I'm now a left-of-center agnostic theist. I grew up mostly in the woods without TV or the internet, then was dropped into the 21st century in college. I've lived in rural America but also in big cities like Atlanta, Los Angeles, and New York. I'm from a poor family in an extremely poor area, but because of my father's blue-collar job at a nearby school, I was lucky enough to go to Syracuse University through a tuition discount. While there, I studied alongside the children of some of the richest families in the country, seeing their lifestyles — and their troubles — firsthand.

I took that Einstein quote to heart at a young age, and I have spent my life since actively seeking a broad range of viewpoints and experiences in the hopes they would give me some insights not only into the problems we're all facing today but also into why the solutions we've tried haven't panned out. I've worked as an actor, a producer, a carpenter, a lifeguard, and a mead brewer. I've labored on demolition crews and for apartment renovation companies. I've coached axe-throwing for tipsy Brooklynites and archery for terminally ill children. I've written TV screenplays and tended bars. I currently work in philosophy as an ethics consultant in AI, and I've done harm-reduction work for Google, Anthropic, and several other companies.

My resume aside, throughout my entire life, my guiding light has been a desire to *understand*. I firmly believe that without truly understanding a problem, our efforts to correct it will be in vain. Naturally, I was drawn to philosophy, though my route was a bit out of the ordinary. I realized early on that a philosophy degree would essentially consist of a guided reading list of public domain works — books I could study on my own. Instead, I chose to go to school for acting. Why? For me, acting was a sort of "philosophy lab." The process of preparing for a role is the process of understanding another person deeply — because you can't play a character you don't understand. Acting school was an opportunity to spend four years practicing empathy for people with different beliefs and backgrounds across a wide range of times and cultures. During that time and after, I never gave up my study of philosophy and history.

Whether or not I agree, I've dedicated my time to understanding where people are coming from — regardless of their backgrounds or political beliefs. In all my time listening to others, I have done so with compassion. And the truth is: both sides of the aisle are hurting. Left or right, if you're working class, things are getting tougher and more uncertain. Upper, middle, or lower class, life is getting more stressful. Now, after years of studying theory and absorbing perspectives from all across the spectrum, I'm ready to start sharing what I've learned.

The truth is our nation's priorities are wildly messed up. The system of capitalist consumerism that we have set up is undermining our country's values and stripping us of our attention spans and self-worth. The left and right each have their pet issues — identity politics, immigration, etc. — but these are simply distractions from the real problem. For all the differences between the sides of the political aisle, most of us can agree on one thing: the America we live in today isn't the one we were promised. Whether you're calling to "Make America Great Again" or to "Never Go Back," you agree that America needs fixing — now is the time to fix it. Contributionism offers a practical solution for the root problem.

Please note — the footnote notations throughout this book are a way to provide additional information without going off on tangents. Many correspond to the bibliography at the end, where you'll find studies, data, or articles to back up my claims. You can feel free to ignore them if you're happy to simply take my word for things (I'm flattered), but I did want to offer further information should you desire it.

THE PHILOSOPHY

We Need a Change

I love this country. Like all countries, the United States has some dark spots in its history, but I believe the goals upon which our nation was founded are noble: that every citizen should have a say. That we should be entitled to life, liberty, and the pursuit of happiness. That people should be free to do and believe what they want — so long as doing so doesn't harm others.

As I mentioned in the foreword, I grew up very conservative and religious. Then, I went out and met a vast array of different people, including many great folks on the left. Both sides are hurting and angry, but at the end of the day, we're all people. At a bedrock level, we mostly want the same things: security for ourselves and our families; the ability to trust our government; to retain our freedoms and make our own choices; to make a better life for ourselves. In short, we want America to live up to its promises.

So, what happened to that? I look around this country and I see millions of hardworking Americans working full-time just to slow their slide into debt. I see learned hopelessness as people set their aims lower and lower. I see a widespread lack of purpose and fulfillment, anxiety and worry about personal and family security, and an understandable cloud of anger and discontentment hanging over all of it.

SO, WHAT'S THE PROBLEM?

The extremist speakers, talk shows, or political parties will point at one cause or another: identity politics, racial injustice, tax rates,

7

economic fears, LGBT rights, immigration concerns, social welfare, or moral decay. Yes, these are important issues, but they're being used as pawns — red herrings to keep us distracted from the real problem. There's a reason everything nowadays is "political." Every issue, even ones that have not historically existed, has been co-opted and inflated, with extremist figures stoking our anger to keep our attention focused on them instead of the root of the problem. (After all, it's a lot easier to rob someone blind if they're not looking.) But the thing at the core? The thing causing so much of our discontentment? Unbridled corporate greed: money-hungry companies, their devaluation of workers' time, and the plastic consumerist culture we've created to secure them more profits. America does have a state religion — it's called consumerist capitalism. The dollar is its God, and it reveres profits, not prophets.

This central issue is like the head of a kraken, and its tentacles can be found tightly wrapped around so many issues in our society.

Are you feeling a lack of fulfillment in your life?

We live in a society where from day one, we're told that our value as human beings comes from the size of our bank account and what we can buy with it. Advertisements, pop culture, and social media bombard us with this message, stripping us of our inherent self-worth and monopolizing our attention to get us to spend more money. As a result, we chase wealth rather than things that will bring us true happiness or fulfillment because we've been convinced that they're the same. In our society, where money equals success, of course, we're feeling unfulfilled.

**Feel like you're throwing your life into work
just to make ends meet?**

Corporations have worked for decades to engineer a "treadmill" that moves at just the right speed to keep you running — and spending — without throwing you off. This is not the relationship we were meant to have with labor. If your job or your life feels like a treadmill, just remember: treadmills were invented as a way of forcing labor out of prisoners.

Feeling disappointed by the educational system?

Wildly low wages mean very little tax money for public school districts. This means underpaid teachers with little access to resources. The wealthy dodge taxes — their kids will go to private schools after all — while the rest of the country must send their own children to underfunded public schools. At the same time, parents are less able to support the teachers' efforts at home — even with a stable two-parent household and only one child, most families still need both parents to work full-time to make ends meet.[1] More time at work means less time (and energy) left for focusing on their child's enrichment. The state of wages in this country means that two-parent households today function like single-parent ones in the 1970s and '80s.

1 It costs about $93k a year to support yourself, a partner, and a single child. The average single income is $59,987/yr. See bibliography for more details.

Feeling disconnected from the people around you?

Social media companies have worked to create an addictive product[2] that offers the illusion of connection and leaves you with nothing. These companies do this because the more time they can get users to spend on their platforms, the more they can charge for advertisements. The result is more isolation, more extremism, and less understanding as our attention and connection with others is mined for profit.

Upset about the environment?

Businesses have been prioritizing profits over sustainability for decades. Meanwhile, these industries pay people to spread bad studies — studies that get shot down by everyone not on the company payroll — and other disinformation to keep the populace confused and voting for the business's interests instead of their own. The result of their focus on short-term profits over the long-term health of our environment is what we're seeing now: extreme weather and natural disasters spurred on by rising global temperatures, costing taxpayers billions in disaster relief. Companies have

---

2 Social media platforms are designed to exploit the part of our brain that makes us feel good when we feel popular — but it replaces real popularity born of meaningful connection with transient popularity born of performativity and entertainment. See bibliography for more.

cut corners to save money and passed the bill on to us. Sorry, Florida.

These problems may appear different on the surface, but if we want to correct our course, it's critical for people to see they all connect. Whenever we get close to identifying the root of these problems — corporate greed — our focus keeps getting pushed by the media (which are massive corporations[3]) toward symptoms and away from the cause itself: the enrichment of the few at the expense of the many, with utter disregard for the future. If we want to have any hope of fixing our communities, our country, and our environment, we need to keep our eyes on the ball.

DIVIDE AND CONQUER

It's important to understand that the right and left are being played off each other so that they don't find their common enemy: exploitation. I'm sick of seeing friends and families working hard at minimum wage or other low-paying jobs for barely enough to scrape by, then seeing that the CEO of their company made $15 million that year. I'm sick of seeing the best people I know treated as nobodies because they chose to devote their lives to improving the world rather than getting rich. And I'm really sick of seeing my friends and family on both sides of the aisle getting hoodwinked into acting against their own long-term interests in the name of the vague concept of "the economy."

---

3 In 1996, media ownership was deregulated by the Telecommunications Act, leading to a consolidation of news ownership. As of 2024, six massive corporations own 90% of news outlets. See bibliography for more.

I have working-class relatives who actually believed in "trickle-down economics" — a policy which claimed that giving tax breaks to the wealthy would enable them to pay their workers more, allowing money to "trickle" back down.[4] Does this make any sense? Are the wealthy just *wishing* they could pay their employees more, if it weren't for those *mean* taxes? No! But it sounded nice enough to fool my relatives into voting against their own interests.

---

4 Trickle-down economics has actually halved our country's economic growth, dropping it from 2.8% yearly in the '60s and '70s to 1.4% yearly from the '80s to present day. See bibliography for more.

Now He Understands The Game

Please note the date. 1916. This isn't new — it has simply been perfected with the rise of streaming services and social media. You'd think we'd have learned by now, but here we are — still distracted and played for fools.

The 2011 Occupy Wall Street movement, though it lacked clear direction or demands, scared the people at the top because, for a moment, Americans started to come together and see corporate greed for the root problem it is. Is it any wonder the media has kept us focused on identity politics ever since? Now, everything is about drawing lines between us based on our "identities," splitting off into little groups, and focusing on ourselves and how we want to be "seen," rather than focusing on the big picture. Instead of one united and powerful group, we've been made into hundreds of little bickering ones. Make no mistake: this is by design. If you can't beat the pack, separate them. We — the bottom 90% — are the pack, and the wealthy-owned political parties and news outlets[5] have done a pretty impressive job of separating us.

THE U.S.A.: A GOVERNMENT "FOR THE (RICH) PEOPLE"

Everything comes back to the first paragraph in this intro: our citizens should be free to do and believe what they want, *so long as doing so doesn't harm others.* America is meant to be a free country. That's one of the ideals that makes it so beautiful. But for any society to function, our freedom to swing our fist *must* end at the tip of another's nose. It's all good fun to wildly fire off a few rounds from a rifle in the morning when you live on a deserted island, but when you live in a small town, that freedom must be given up for the safety of others. When people prove that they *can't* behave responsibly and treat others well on their own — that's when laws become necessary.

Our government has a responsibility to make and use laws to look out for its citizens; that's the whole purpose of government. This means *all* citizens. Yet, because of our two-party system and the way campaigns are financed, they look out for some citizens — the wealthy ones — far more than others. An easy example of this is using flat fines to punish bad behavior; in American society, your freedom to swing your fist is virtually unlimited, provided you have the money. The world we've created is the logical result of decades of politicians looking out for the few with money instead of citizens as a whole. Decades of promoting the

---

5 Through campaign finance policies like those pushed for by Citizens United (which I'll go into more later on) and the near monopolization of the news, the wealthy own both politicians and the news.

interests of business over the interests of the people as a whole.[6] If we want to solve our problems, we must demand that politicians prioritize the people once more and focus on using law to keep business fair, honest, and responsible; big business has certainly proven it won't be fair, honest, and responsible on its own.

GOOD INTENTIONS GONE AWRY

This may trigger some of my left-leaning readers, but I actually love the sentiment behind the slogan "Make America Great." This is an excellent goal; after all, we are in dire need of some improvement. But I've always had an issue with the fact that it doesn't specify what "great" means. My grandfather was a navigator in WW2, and my father was a scoutmaster. One lesson I learned young is that if you don't have a solid destination in mind, you'll never get where you're trying to go. So, while I'm on board with the idea of making America "great," I also know that we need to be a little more specific if we want any hope of reaching our destination.

What if we lived in a country where, if you're working a full-time job, you can buy a home and not worry about healthcare? Would that not be "great"? The jobs are clearly worth doing because businesses eat into their profits to hire someone to do it. Would it not be "great" if being a hard-working citizen in the U.S. guaranteed you the ability to live comfortably and enjoy a good life?

What if we lived in a country where both parents didn't need to work full-time to support a child? Where parents have more time to support the efforts of teachers and to take a more active role in their children's development?

---

6 Examples of this include sugar industry subsidies, bailouts of failing corporations using taxpayer dollars, and siding with big oil companies on carbon-pricing measures. See bibliography for more.

Or where it doesn't feel like our entire purpose in life is to earn pennies from the rich person we work for, just to give them all to the rich person we rent from? Where we can work a job and still have time and money left over to pursue the passions that make life worth living in the first place?

So, how can we accomplish this? Some folks always suggest raising the minimum wage, which is at best a Band-Aid®. Businesses attempt to make up their profits by raising prices and the treadmill keeps spinning — it just moves a little faster.

Many economic theories and fixes have been tried, and they have all fallen to corruption and greed. But what if there was a theory that used human psychology and realism to create a system in which hard work was both encouraged *and* rewarded? Allow me to humbly present my solution (this is the manifesto part):

CONTRIBUTIONISM

Contributionism is a philosophy that seeks to unite ethics with practical business while avoiding unrealistic idealism. It's the radical concept that, if you're spending your valuable time contributing to a company's operation, you should be fairly compensated for giving the company that chunk of your life. Likewise, contributionism states that if you're making money from the work of other people, you should not be reaping a disproportionate amount of the fruits of their labor. Most importantly, as I'll say many times in this book: contributionism doesn't require an entire overhaul of the system — simply a change to the way a business compensates its employees and investors.

It should be noted that the term "contributionism" does exist — something I discovered during my research for this book. It isn't well defined; it's more of a general concept with a focus on community and ecology than a fleshed-out economic system. My version of contributionism — Fiskian contributionism if you will — is more complete and more actionable, and it deals primarily with economics. Throughout this book, when I mention contributionism, I'll be talking about this economic system rather than the general philosophy.

We'll be going into a more detailed description of how contributionism works and the nitty-gritty in just a moment. First, however, we need to discuss some basic philosophy to ensure we're on the same page about two fundamental concepts.

A LIFE IS MADE UP OF TIME

Point one is simple. Every person has one type of resource in common: time. Regardless of class, race, background, or beliefs, each person has the exact same number of minutes in each day, and every person's minute is the same length. These minutes are the most precious resource that we have—because one day, each of us will run out of them. In the meantime, they can be spent working, pursuing passions, making memories, and otherwise sucking the marrow from this limited life of ours.

That's it for point one. Easy peasy. If we can all agree and acknowledge that the most valuable resource a person has is their time then we're ready to move on to the next point.

SUPERMAN IS JUST A COMIC BOOK CHARACTER

For point two, let's talk about the human capacity to work. If you've lived in the U.S. of A. for the past decade, you've seen a flood of superhero movies. These are fun popcorn flicks, sure, but they don't represent real life. Superman is able to throw an entire train like it's a roll of toilet paper, and Lex Luthor is able to plan 132 steps ahead, but I hope I don't need to remind my readers that these characters aren't real. So, let's take a moment to examine reality.

Looking at strength, if we use deadlifts as a measurement, the strongest man in the world is only about six times stronger than an average man. IQ is a controversial and subjective way of measuring intelligence, but in theory, a person who scores a 200 on a psychiatrist-administered test would have a brain that is twice as powerful as an average person (someone with an IQ of 100). The highest credibly recorded IQ belonged to Marilyn vos Savant, who had an IQ of 227. Even far-fetched and untested claims don't range above about 400, which, if they're true, would be four times greater than an average person.

The point of all this is simply that, given similar effort, resources, and experience, one person cannot accomplish ten times as much as another person. In one hour, if two people with similar instructions are both putting in effort — whether it's digging a hole, writing emails, or making coffee — one person would have difficulty doing three times as much as the other, much less ten times more. Imagine that two able-bodied men are loading bricks into trucks by hand. If it takes one person an hour to do it, would it be possible for the other to load his truck in six minutes? Of course not. Unless one of them uses a machine, in which case it's the machine that makes the difference, not work ethic.

Some folks will inevitably point out that people don't always give their all. Hard workers may do far more work than lazy ones. This is a valid concern, and it's a reality that contributionism seeks to acknowledge. Ultimately, hard work comes down to motivation, and the pay rates at many companies across the country are anything but motivational. After all, if you *could* afford to pay employees more, how can you pay them minimum wage and ask for maximum effort? We'll get into how contributionism provides this motivation in more detail later on, but for now, all I'm asking you to accept is this: if two people with similar training focus on doing the same task, one person cannot accomplish ten times as much as the other.

This is an important reality that we need to understand before moving further. If you still have reservations on this point, consider that even hugely successful business tycoons accomplish what they do by telling others what work to do. They are "successful" because they have positioned themselves at the head of a huge network of individuals who are all giving their time and energy to facilitate the company's success.

When a successful businessperson employs 100 people, each working 8-hour days, that businessperson effectively gets an extra 800 hours a day.

And that's it. So far, the only facts that I've asked you, dear reader, to accept are that time is the most valuable asset any person has, and that given the same amount of time and similar resources, experience, and motivation, one able-bodied person cannot do ten times as much work as another.

FOLLOW THE MONEY

Before we jump too deep into this, I want to get clear on a word I'll be using a lot: "wealthy." When I refer to "the wealthy," I'm talking about the top 10% of the population in terms of net worth. These are *individuals* who are making over $170k each year, according to numbers from the Social Security Administration.[7] This top 10% of the nation holds 70% of our nation's wealth — leaving 30% of the wealth for the other 90%.[8] Want to guess how much wealth the bottom 50% holds? About 2.5%.[9] I'll touch on this more later, but I wanted to give some sort of definition of whom I'm referring to when I say, "the wealthy." If you're making $125k a year, I'm likely not talking about you.

---

7 There is a *huge* range in income within the top 10% of earners. However, the Social Security Administration considers $173k the average, so I'm using $170k here. See bibliography for a more in-depth breakdown.

8 This is the problem we're facing. Money has been drained from communities as most of the profits from the mega-corporations they shop at are sent back to wealthy owners and shareholders living far away. See bibliography for more details.

9 Why can't you afford things? It isn't just the cost of goods — it's the fact that your money has been siphoned away. See bibliography for more details.

Now, remembering the two points we discussed above, let's take a look at business — especially corporate business — in the United States today. Let's make up a fictional corporate coffee chain. We'll call it Ahab's. It's a big competitor of Starbucks. What would happen if we divided the employees of Ahab's Coffee so that everybody in corporate is above the line and everyone "in the field" is below the line? If we removed the corporate half, people would still get their coffee. There may be supply chain mix-ups and some inefficiency at first, but business would eventually get back on track as individual locations found their footing. People would still get their coffee, and Ahab's would still be a functional chain. But, if you remove the "in the field" half of the company, nobody is getting their coffee. The business ceases to function. Even if the corporate half jumped behind the counters, they would come in having little experience actually making coffee, and given how small a percentage of the company is corporate, they wouldn't even have the personnel to staff half their locations.

Contributionism asks, "If the people on the ground floor are the ones doing the necessary work to actually make the company run, why are the people at the top making the vast majority of the money that their work generates?" When one person works for another, that person is giving a portion of their life to facilitate the success of their employer's business. As a trade, the employer pays them money for their contribution of time. Recall point number one that we discussed above — in this trade, the employee is providing the more valuable resource. But we've been tricked, gaslit into believing our time is less valuable than it really is. We can see the value of our work because it generates enough revenue to pay higher-ups in the company millions every year while still leaving profits for investors. But since the 1970s, these companies have repeatedly decided it's fair and reasonable to claim a larger and larger chunk of the rewards of our labor,[10] keeping the pay for the bottom relatively low and receiving more and more money themselves.

IF A JOB IS WORTH DOING, IT DESERVES TO BE PAID FAIRLY

Ultimately, money represents goods and services — including the things necessary to sustain or improve our lives. It isn't everything and it can't buy happiness — but money *can* facilitate happiness when it rids you of uncertainty and the stress of not being able to afford necessities. Even an overnight parking garage attendant who usually has little to do is giving a chunk of their limited time to make money for their boss — they should be given at least enough money to sustain themselves and afford a reasonable quality of life in exchange for that time.

Clients often disrespect catering staff — I know, having worked as a catering server in NYC — but without them, you're serving the whole event yourself. A caterer's hour is just as long as yours. If you want them to do the job, shouldn't they be able to live a secure life without needing to work 50 hours a week?

It all comes down to this: if a job is important enough to have someone do it, it's important enough to pay them fairly for their time. Remember: bosses only hire people when they think the worker will earn more than they cost. They know the job is valuable — if you're being paid nothing compared to them, it's because the bosses have tricked you into thinking your work — and time — is less valuable than it is.

---

10 As productivity has risen, wages at the bottom have stayed roughly the same, while the earnings from those at the top have skyrocketed. See bibliography for more details.

THE MARVEL OF CEOS: SELF-DECLARED SUPERHUMANS

That brings us right back to point number two that we talked about earlier. How can a CEO claim that an hour of their time is worth hundreds of times more than that of their entry-level employees? They can't be doing hundreds of times more work in that hour. Any decision they make that makes the company money is just a direction to others — who then do the actual work. Perhaps this does deserve some extra compensation — I'm not debating its value. But a 30x difference is extortionate, much less hundreds of times.

This is textbook time theft and exploitation, with a side of gaslighting to keep us from realizing that we're in an abusive relationship. The fact that our most precious possession — our lives — are being stolen from us should enrage the American working class. But the slide into this exploitation has been slow and accompanied by misinformation, politicking, and flashy media that distracts us from the real issues plaguing us. Instead of having bread and circuses, we now have fast food and streaming.

To really lay this out — when I say CEOs are receiving hundreds of times what their ground-level employees are making, that number isn't an exaggeration. According to the Economic Policy Institute, CEOs' realized compensation (which includes pay, bonuses, and company stocks) increased during the COVID-19 pandemic, putting the average CEO:worker compensation ratio at 344:1 in 2022. In 1965 — presumably, when America was "Great" — the ratio was about 21:1,[11] giving American workers the ability to thrive and secure better lives for themselves. But, since the late '70s, average realized compensation for

---

11 This trend of rising CEO pay and stagnating worker pay began slowly in the late '70s, sped up in the '80s, and rocketed through the roof in the '90s. See bibliography for more details.

CEOs increased by *1,209.2%* from 1978 to 2022,[10] significantly outpacing inflation. Want to know how much the average worker's annual compensation rose in that time? 15.3%.[10]

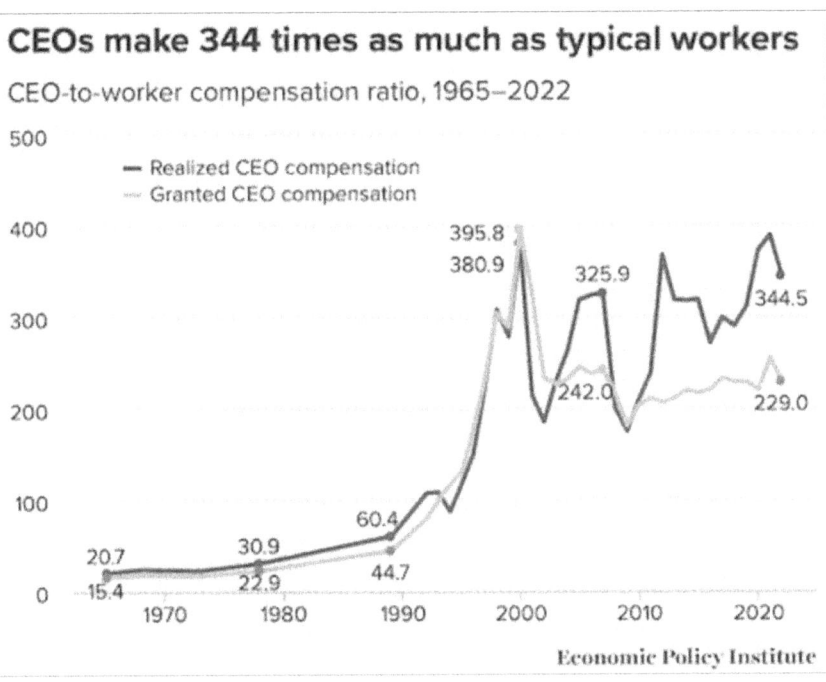

CEOs make 344 times as much as typical workers

CEO-to-worker compensation ratio, 1965–2022

Does this mean that CEOs now are *twelve times* (that's 1,200%) more valuable, or that they contribute twelve times more than their counterparts in the '70s? Of course not. They've just gotten better at using their power to increase their own compensation and worse at respecting and appreciating the hours of life that their workers are sacrificing for their enrichment. This is supported by the numbers: productivity is up by 80% since 1978,[12] yet typical workers are only

---

12 "Since the late 1970s, our policy choices have led directly to a pronounced divergence between productivity and typical workers' pay. But it didn't have to be this way... Starting in the late 1970s policymakers began dismantling all the policy bulwarks helping to ensure that typical workers' wages grew with productivity." - Excerpt from the EPI article "The Productivity–Pay Gap". It's an excellent article that goes into the policy decisions behind this. See bibliography for citation and details.

being paid slightly more; the money from that extra productivity is going to the top instead of to them. This is how executives are able to receive such a huge increase in compensation — the pie is getting larger, but the numbers show that executives and investors are keeping more of the pie for themselves and giving less to the workers who made it. And I don't know about you, but I love pie. Apple pie with a nice lattice crust? Delicious. If I help make that pie, I'm sure as hell going to want my fair share of it.

I FOUND YOUR HOUSE!

All of these numbers can be a bit meaningless on their own, so let's look at a concrete example. Assuming a 50-week work year, the average annual pay for workers in 1979 was $12,050.[13] Keep in mind: this is working-class pay, very often with no higher education. Adjusted for inflation, that's $52,209/year in 2024 dollars.

If wages rose at the same rate as productivity (which again, rose by 80%[11]), the average worker's pay today should be $93,976/year. Instead, it's $59,987.[2] That's a missing $33,989 each year. $33,989 per person of extra product that workers are making each year compared to their counterparts in 1979. $33,989 that they aren't seeing a penny of — that's going straight into the pockets of corporate and shareholders. In ten years of this, a worker is robbed of $339,890 worth of productivity.

Now — we're currently seeing a massive decline in homeownership as working-class people are priced out of the market… and the average cost of a home in the U.S. as of August 2024 is $406,100.[14] There's your

---

[13] A Bureau of Labor Statistics table including average weekly worker pay throughout the years can be found in the bibliography.

[14] Obviously, it depends on where you live, but this was the average across the U.S. See bibliography for more details.

house. The problem isn't housing availability, spending habits, or a lack of higher education — it's the fact that a working-class American has the cost of a home stolen from the value of their labor every thirteen years. This is the problem. Not tax rates or support for social welfare programs.

Replace "Pullman" with "Amazon" or any modern mega-corporation and it works today.

All these tax-funded "fixes" — universal basic income, universal healthcare, social welfare programs, etc. — are "backend fixes." They're all attempts to address issues *after* they arise, instead of preventing them in the first place. If people are paid fairly for the contribution of their work, they can afford healthcare on their own. If working a full-time job made you enough to buy a home and support a family (as it did in the

'60s to the '80s) we wouldn't need social welfare programs nearly as much. Implementing contributionism addresses the cause of the problem rather than the symptoms of the problem. To make an analogy: if the problem is a cut, social welfare is a Band-Aid® — but contributionism is avoiding the cut in the first place.

This brings us to the meat of what contributionism is. At its core, contributionism is an attempt to bring morality, ethics, and business together. Acknowledging the two facts I laid out above — that people's time is valuable and that their labor is not insignificant — contributionism states that the highest-paid person in a company should not be allowed to make more than ten times as much as their ground-level employees. This ratio decreases as you go down through the company, with middle-level management able to make five times as much as an entry-level employee and so forth.

A LOOK AT ECONOMICS

The beauty of contributionism is that it marries the ethics of communism with the practicality of capitalism. Now don't jump down my throat for saying the word "communism." I'll be the first to say that it has plenty of issues. In fact, both of these philosophies have shortcomings of their own — shortcomings that have been well documented throughout history. Let's take a look at each.

COMMUNISM: IDEALISM AS ECONOMICS

Communism. It's a scary word for many, and one with a lot of baggage attached. Don't worry though, this is not a pro-communist book.

First, what even is communism? Communism is a form of government based on the principles of the philosophy of Marxism, as laid out by Karl Marx. Marxism itself is based on a noble goal — for the efforts of all people to be appreciated equally and for their work to be rewarded. It's the whole "from each according to their ability, to each according to their need" that you were quizzed on in history class. This is all well and good in theory, but historically, it doesn't work when it's put into practice on a large scale and inevitably becomes communism.

By rewarding all effort equally, communism removes all incentive to work harder and try harder. When you get the same as everyone else — regardless of how hard you work — there is no tangible reason to work harder or aspire for greater things. The unmotivated drain resources and morale from the driven, and the whole country gradually declines.[15]

---

[15] It is idealistic to believe that everyone will simply band together and give it their all. Idealism is all well and good — it is the compass we use to guide our progress. But a

Beyond this economic decline, communism leads to rapid corruption — when individuals are put in charge of the allocation of resources, it doesn't take long for those individuals to begin abusing their power. Who decides how much each person must give? Who decides how much each person needs? Or as George Orwell might put it, while all animals are equal, who decides which animals are more equal than others? This is an immense amount of power, and power corrupts absolutely.

All of this should be taken with a grain of salt, of course — the U.S. spent decades toppling governments that had communist leanings. We'll never know how those countries would have turned out because they didn't get a chance to develop. However, given what we've seen in large-scale communist countries that *have* had the chance to develop, there's no reason to assume these countries would have grown into a corruption-free paradise. We need look no further than the Soviet Union or Maoist China's "Great Leap Forward" for examples.

These are the shortcomings of communism in a nutshell. I didn't spend much time on it because we've all heard the arguments against it growing up in the U.S. of A. Talking about problems with our beloved capitalism is a bit harder…

CAPITALISM: ALSO IDEALISM AS ECONOMICS

So, what's the issue with capitalism? This is a little trickier to explain because capitalist economies and governments evolve over time. The early stage is admittedly great, but the late phase has inspired entire dystopian genres (see: Cyberpunk). A quick clarification for the economic theory nerds out there: In this book, I'll be referring to the phases of this cycle as "early-stage capitalism" and "late-stage

---

system based solely on idealism is doomed to fail. We must acknowledge reality. See bibliography for more details.

capitalism." These terms are also used in economic history to describe different historical epochs, but I'll be using them for my own purposes in this book. On with the show.

I'm not going to lie to you; early-stage capitalism is amazing. This is the period after a major shift, like a "burn it down" style revolution, a big war, or the founding of a new country. People have similar levels of resources compared to late-stage capitalism, there are private businesses and ventures everywhere, and employers pay higher wages because they're competing for good workers. Nike, Dell, and Hewlett-Packard are just a few examples of companies that got their start during early-stage capitalism. This economic environment leads to greater social mobility and the ability to improve your lot in life if you work hard. This mobility allows more people to start their own businesses, creating market competition and ensuring high-quality products and services. It's everything your most economically conservative uncle says capitalism is. It's a really great time. The problem is, if left unchecked, early-stage capitalism inevitably leads to late-stage capitalism.

HOW DOES LATE-STAGE CAPITALISM HAPPEN?

Late-stage capitalism — or "corporate capitalism" — is what happens once wealth has consolidated to the point that small business is choked out, and the wealthy can make more off their stock market investments each year than an average person's annual income. It's what naturally happens when enough time and generations pass in a society that runs on the principle "it takes money to make money." After all, a venture requires resources.

During early-stage capitalism, some folks inevitably find great success. This success is due to some combination of six factors: connections, hard work, intellect/vision, talent, good fortune, and — very importantly — access to resources. This access to resources is important because not only are resources required to start a venture, but they also serve as a "wild card" — they can be used as a crutch to supplement any of the other factors. With enough resources, a person doesn't need to work hard; they can pay someone else to. They don't need to be clever or skillful — they can hire brilliant and talented people who need the money. They can use the influence that vast resources provide to make connections they otherwise wouldn't have. And nothing fixes bad luck like throwing a stack of money at it.

In the beginning, the playing field is — relatively — level. Some people find success as a result of their skill, luck, and work ethic. As a result of their success, these individuals are able to pass on greater resources to their children. These resources mean their children's success is less dependent on hard work and fortune than their parents' or their peers who have access to less. Assuming these children aren't utterly incompetent and don't suffer a disaster, they'll have a much easier time making more money than their poorer contemporaries and will thus provide even greater pools of resources to their own children. Their children, in turn, will have an even higher likelihood of success, regardless of their ingenuity or work ethic. When you start a marathon at the halfway point, it's much easier to get a good finishing time.

This cycle is accelerated when an economy includes corporations. With corporate capitalism, a wealthy person can simply give startup money to a venture and then profit off that venture in perpetuity, despite never having done any actual work for the company. If you've worked "below the line" for a large-scale corporation in the past decade, it's likely that several large shareholders made more from your work each year than you did, without ever leaving their yachts, because years or decades ago they gave money to the company — or their parents did. With this dividend income, the children of the wealthy can go their entire lives without working, making more money than an average American worker simply from the dividends generated by the stock portfolio or trust fund their parents gave them.[16] They make a better living than most hardworking blue-collar workers simply by leeching profits from the people earning them.[17]

As this cycle goes on, wealth continues to consolidate, and a poor person has more and more difficulty starting their own business. For them, a business requires a risky loan. After the loan is taken out, they are on the hook to repay it, and they must do so while competing with larger, better-established companies with massive resources and manufacturing behind them. If they don't succeed, they stand to lose everything.

Because of this risk, small businesses become more and more scarce, which means so do job options. And as these options decrease, companies are able to pay their employees less and less — because it's either take what they offer or be unemployed. This, in turn, gives workers in the lower classes fewer and fewer resources, making entrepreneurship more and more difficult, and accelerating the cycle.

Give this cycle enough time, and eventually, you have what we see in the U.S. right now: Millions of our fellow citizens live hand to mouth, forced to pick between food, rent, and healthcare because their

---

16 The ultra-wealthy make 47.21% of their income from investments alone. That's a massive amount of money — hundreds of thousands of dollars. Wages (which make up most income from the bottom 98% of earners) are taxed more heavily than capital gains, meaning the ultra-wealthy get to pay less taxes on their idle income. See bibliography for citation and details.

17 According to a report published in 2024, since the Trump-GOP tax laws were passed in 2017, business stockholder payouts have totaled $4.4 trillion. Meanwhile, businesses paid only $608 billion in taxes. This has led to crumbling public services and government instability as well as stagnating worker wages, all while wealthy shareholders surge ahead on profits from their workers' labor. See bibliography for full report.

employers pay them a fraction of what their work is worth.[18] There are a shameful number of people working full-time who can hardly afford their basic necessities, let alone contributing to savings for the inevitable challenges life throws at us. In fact, as of 2020, *70% of people on food stamps or Medicaid had a full-time job.*[19] Perhaps they can eventually scrape together enough to buy a home, but not if they hope to retire or if they want to save money for unforeseen medical expenses.[20] At the same time, you see their executives and majority shareholders buying mansions and yachts and raking in money at an ever-increasing rate.

YOU SAY CAPITALISM, I SAY OLIGARCHY

When you understand that in capitalism it's easier to make money the more money you have, it's easy to see why late-stage capitalism — if left unchecked — will always evolve into its final form: oligarchy. A government officially run by the wealthy, for the wealthy. In 2025, we're currently somewhere between late-stage capitalism and oligarchy. The wealthy don't formally and openly run the country (as of 2024 — though it looks like that could be changing[21]), but they do own the politicians

---

18 A recent study by the National Low Income Housing Coalition found that there isn't a single congressional district in the country where a full-time minimum wage worker could afford a two-bedroom apartment. See bibliography for citation and details.

19 There is a myth pushed by pro-corporate elites that people on social welfare like food stamps or Medicaid are simply lazy. Data shows that for many, this isn't the case — it's simply that their full-time wages are too low for them to live on. See bibliography for more details.

20 In 2024, nearly 30% of American households lived paycheck to paycheck, with their necessity spending greater than 90% of their income. See bibliography for more details.

21 With the institution of the "Department Of Government Efficiency," the ultra-wealthy now have unprecedented direct control over the government and all its policies. Remember — they're the ones

that do (through campaign finance), as well as the news outlets that "inform" (misdirect) the public — and most people realize it on some level.

If, for some reason, you haven't been paying attention to the laws in this country and you don't believe me, look up "corporate personhood"[22] and "limited liability."[23] Then, explain to me how, in a country that's supposed to be "for the people," policies have been passed to make it difficult for the owners of companies to face consequences for any damage their company causes *to* the people. This country is for the people — so business interests have pushed at every turn to make corporations people in order to shield the owners from responsibility[24] and exercise even more power over elections and politicians.[25]

An excellent concrete example of how this all works — how wealthy individuals and businesses can essentially "buy" politicians — is the Supreme Court case of Citizens United v. the Federal Election

---

not paying people in the first place; that's how they got rich. They aren't looking to help The People — they're looking to help themselves.

22 This law allows businesses to be recognized as individuals, extending to them all the legal protections and benefits that a human citizen gets, protecting those running the business from consequences. See bibliography for more details.

23 Also called the "corporate shield doctrine." As in, legally shielding yourself from consequences of your business's actions. See bibliography for more details.

24 This idea of "corporate personhood" has been evolving for a long time, granting greater and greater personhood (and the protections that come with it) to business. See bibliography for citation and details.

25 Corporations are using the 1st Amendment to push voters out of the central role in our election process, by treating corporate political spending as protected speech. See bibliography for more details.

Commission, back in 2010.[26] Citizens United is a large conservative nonprofit organization whose goal is to minimize government while maximizing private business' control over the American populace. They aim to do this by weakening government regulation so that private business owners can do just about whatever they want to their employees (and our planet and society) in the name of personal profit for a handful of people at the top.

In the 2010 case, Citizens United claimed that restrictions on businesses giving money to political campaigns are unconstitutional, and the Supreme Court (Republican-controlled at the time) agreed. As a result, corporations are allowed to spend an unlimited amount of money on political advertising. This means that if a politician wants to be elected (or re-elected) they must do as corporations wish — because if they don't, those corporations can dump tens of millions of dollars into the campaign advertisements for their competition. This naturally means that the majority of our politicians are quite friendly with corporate interests.

Bernie Sanders attempted to get around this in 2016 by running a largely crowdfunded campaign, but the Democratic National Committee violated their own stated neutrality to support Hillary Clinton's nomination (really "showing their hand" when it comes to who they actually work for).

Through corrupt campaign finance policies, mega-corporations collectively spend hundreds of millions of dollars annually[26] to influence campaigns and spread propaganda. They do this so that they can get people into power who will work for them, rather than for the American masses. To add insult to injury, if you're a worker, these millions of dollars are dollars that *your work* generated! This is all money that came

---

26 Since this decision, we have seen the creation of "Super PACs" and a massive ballooning in corporate spending on elections. See bibliography for information, and the impact this has had.

from your work, which you aren't seeing because it's being used to manipulate your political system.

To make matters worse, through this campaign financing, the mega-wealthy class has recently gained unprecedented direct control over our government and its operations. We're like a flock of sheep being mysteriously killed off by predators in the night, who voted to put wolves in charge to stop the killings — simply because the wolves promised they would.

CONSUMERIST CAPITALISM: TRADING PERSONAL VALUE FOR PERSONAL PROFIT

We've beaten this horse pretty dead, but one final point against capitalism that people don't discuss as much as I'd like: beyond leading to financial inequality and desperation, late-stage capitalism strips people of their value as individuals. Your worth as a human being becomes your bank account balance. If you want anyone to think you're worth anything, you have to show your wealth by continuously buying the "right" designer products: a Rolex, Air Jordans, designer clothes, expensive makeup or jewelry, fancy cars and houses, etc.

This "money = personal value" mentality sells a lot of products and makes a lot of money for the owners of businesses. But when all is said and done, consumerism is just a marketing tactic — one that erodes the character and values of the nation[27] and forces its citizens to give money

---

27 There is a long but excellent article called "A New Hedonism: A Post-Consumerism Vision" that begins by outlining how this hurts everyone - both the working class and the wealthy. See bibliography.

to rich business owners in order to be seen by others, and themselves, as worthy. It's your classic "Snob Appeal Fallacy" nonsense.

Who cares if you're a teacher who volunteers at their local soup kitchen twice a week? You're not wearing a designer label, so how can you possibly be as important or valuable as a trendy influencer who makes tons of money by doing dances on social media? How could you possibly deserve the same respect as a CEO who boosted company profits by moving manufacturing to a sweatshop in Indonesia?

In the same way that communism strips citizens of the motivation to be productive, capitalism strips its citizens of the motivation to be good, nuanced people. Not only is "goodness" not rewarded to the same degree as wealth, but being a good, moral person often gets in the way if your desire is to become mega-rich. Paying everyone well, caring about the wellbeing of the public, working to make the environment safer — none of these things will help you to become a billionaire.

Beyond this value distortion, the consumerist mindset that late-stage capitalism promotes strips the depth and joy from our lives by teaching us to pursue the accumulation of trivial consumer goods instead of things that bring us lasting happiness and fulfillment. We'll go more into the science behind this shortly, but for now, it's important to understand that the consumerist culture we've created dissolves the very bedrock on which living a good life is built.[28]

---

28 Technological and social advances have led to greater dissatisfaction with life - so much so that self-care has been monetized and changed from preservation to consumption. See bibliography for more.

AMERICAN CAPITALISM: WELFARE FOR BUSINESS, FEUDALISM FOR WORKERS

It's worth noting that — in addition to the issues I've stated above — our current version of capitalism isn't even a proper free market. A free market is just what it sounds like: businesses are free to succeed or fail based on their decisions and those of the consumer. In America, however, companies receive government funds in the form of bailouts and tax breaks (a penny saved is a penny earned, yes?). Many businesses aren't allowed to fail if they do poorly — if they're big enough, the government simply takes money from the citizens' wallets and gives it to the business so that it can continue to stagger along, all while the management responsible continues to receive massive paychecks.[29]

The COVID-19 pandemic itself saw billions of taxpayer dollars funneled from hardworking Americans experiencing economic stress directly to large corporations, who then paid their CEOs millions — and majority shareholders billions — while at the same time laying off thousands of employees. Exxon, Honeywell, and Coca-Cola are just a few examples.[30] This isn't a free market. It's taking money from the American People to provide handouts to businesses. This is welfare for the rich.

While corporations and the wealthy who run them receive welfare from the pockets of the working class, many of those workers live in a form of modern feudalism. According to the U.S. Census Bureau, homeownership is slowing as more and more people are renting as they're priced out of the housing market or outbid by large real estate companies.[31] At the same time, the cost of goods and rent are rising and

---

29 See bibliography for a supporting article, note especially the "Creation of Moral Hazard and Too-Big-to-Fail Competitive Advantage" section.

30 More on this, including specific offenders, can be found in the bibliography.

31 Due to the rising cost of housing driven by these companies, in 2024, we experienced the lowest homeownership rate in four years. See bibliography for more information.

wages aren't keeping up — *someone* is making money off of these price increases, but the folks at the bottom doing the work aren't seeing it.

Because of the rising cost of housing and decreasing wages, we've wound up with a system where many people work full-time to make just enough to afford rent and modest comforts, with little hope of saving up.[32] For quite a few, one surprise expense is all it would take to bury them in debt — in fact, a 2022 Federal Reserve survey indicated that 37% of Americans would be unable to pay a surprise $400 expense without borrowing, using credit, or selling some property.[33]

This is late-stage capitalism doing an impression of medieval feudalism.[34] Humor me as we explore this comparison — in feudalism, a noble owns land, which the tenants are legally bound to. These tenants provide labor to the noble in exchange for the noble's protection and the right to live on the land. Nowadays, landlords own apartments. Their tenants are not legally bound to their "land," but rather financially bound to it due to the high cost of living and low wages. After all, if someone is living paycheck to paycheck with no savings, a new security deposit and moving costs could be enough to drive them into debt. Yes, these modern "rent serfs" work for someone other than their landlord, but by being paid barely enough to stay afloat, they still end up bound — simply by lack of funds rather than law. It's feudalism with a middleman.

---

32 More than a third of Americans are living paycheck to paycheck. See bibliography for more data.

33 A repetition of what I mentioned earlier, but see bibliography for *even more* data, this time from the Federal Reserve Board.

34 The term in philosophical circles is "Neo-Feudalism." See bibliography for an article and book recommendation.

THE PSYCHOLOGY OF THE PROBLEM

GREED: THE WORM IN THE APPLE

*R*egardless of the economic system, it always succumbs to corruption and abuse, with a select few wealthy people using their power to exploit those beneath them for personal gain. We discussed communism and capitalism, but this trend also applies to mercantilism, feudalism, and ancient command economies. This corruption is most often driven by greed — the greed of government officials, the greed of businesses, or a mix. It makes a lot of sense. Greed is present throughout humanity, which means its effects have influenced all economic systems. But what is greed? It's a word that gets thrown around a lot without being fully considered — and it isn't as simple as "wanting more."

Imagine a catered meal at an event. If a person gets their first plate of food, are they greedy? No, they haven't eaten yet, they're hungry, and it's understood that everyone gets a plate of food. But what about when they want seconds? Well, if everyone has had their first plate already, that isn't greedy. Even if some folks have not gotten their first plate yet, if there is clearly no risk of running out, it still isn't greedy because nobody is being deprived of food. However, if some folks haven't gotten their first plate yet and food is running low, then a person grabbing another plate *is* being greedy — their excess is depriving others of their fair share.

So, greed can be defined as "taking more for yourself when you already have enough, to the detriment of others." I really want to stress the importance of that last part: *"to the detriment of others."*

We've seen greed crop up repeatedly throughout history, ruining economies and societies since time immemorial.[35] It's one of the great unifying human traditions. Why is that? What drives this greed on the part of those who already have enough? It's easily explained when you understand our deep past. Our ancestors didn't have deadly claws or thick skin to help them survive. Instead, they used intelligence and cunning to deal with their problems. One way they did this was by preparing for the future, by accumulating and storing resources in preparation for the next famine, or drought, or winter.

Over the many, many generations throughout history, this was "programmed" into us as instinct through the use of a chemical "reward system" in our brains.

---

35 As an example, look at every society that colonialism decimated for profit. For more specific examples, check out The Great Famine (1315–1317), The Price Revolution (16th century), The South Sea and Mississippi Bubbles (1720s), The Great Financial Crisis of 1914, and The Enron Scandal (2001). These are just a handful to get you started.

THE SCIENCE OF HAPPINESS

This isn't a neuroscience textbook, so I'm simplifying a bit, but our "animal brain" (the subconscious part of our mind) wants us *and* our pack to survive. In order to reward behaviors that give us better chances of personal or pack survival, our brain releases "pleasure chemicals". The big three are dopamine, serotonin, and oxytocin.[36] Each feels a bit different, and each is triggered by different things.

> **Serotonin** is the "happiness hormone." It stabilizes our mood and makes us feel content and happy with life in a more long-term way. It's released largely through exercise and positive experiences.
>
> **Oxytocin** is the "love hormone," and it makes us feel both platonic and romantic love, as well as allowing us to give and receive kindness. It's released largely in response to things like positive social interactions and physical touch.
>
> **Dopamine** is the "reward hormone." It makes us feel good for a brief time when we feel we've accomplished something and motivates us to do it again. This feeling of "accomplishment" can come from doing a job well or achieving a goal — but it can also come from simply accumulating more things. Back in the day, accumulation usually meant food or other much-needed resources, but in the modern world, it often means a new item or more money — *whether we actually need it or not.*

The effect of dopamine is the psychological explanation for greed: accumulation presses an ancient "button" in our brain, releasing a hit of

---

36 Endorphins are also important neurotransmitters, though they are associated with pain relief. See bibliography for more in-depth reading on the subject of our happiness hormones

dopamine as a reward, which makes us feel good until it dissipates.[37] To get the next hit of dopamine, we must accumulate again. This instinctual feature helped our ancestors to survive in an uncertain world with limited resources, but it's still present within us today — whether we're actually at risk of scarcity or not. It feels great, which tends to make it highly addictive — the term for it is "accumulation addiction" or "wealth addiction."[38] In fact, cocaine addiction operates in a similar way — the drug floods the brain with dopamine, and users need to keep using it to get their fix.[39] This explains why greed is such an intrinsic part of human nature and why it can never be satisfied — the *objects* of wealth are not what bring happiness, simply the *act of accumulating* those objects.

This act of repeatedly chasing dopamine through accumulation only gives temporary, hollow happiness. It makes sense — dopamine is a short-lived "feel good hormone." It doesn't provide the feelings of lasting happiness and contentment that serotonin provides, and it doesn't provide the feelings of love, connection, or community that oxytocin provides. The tricky part is, while serotonin and oxytocin are released by activities that take more effort and care, dopamine can simply be bought. This is why the "miserable rich person" is such a common trope — dopamine is an easy neurotransmitter to get, and it makes you feel temporarily happy, but it can lead a person to neglect the things that provide long-term happiness and fulfillment. It's like a person chasing

---

37 This cycle drives addictive behaviors, and it is consciously used by companies to get us to buy more. See bibliography for more info on exactly how.

38 See bibliography for two articles on spending addiction and wealth addiction.

39 See bibliography for an article on cocaine addiction from the *Journal of Neuroscience*. Please do feel free to compare the effects of cocaine on the dopamine system with the effects of spending and wealth referenced in bibliography 38.

fleeting happiness from likes on social media while neglecting real social connections.

Hey, rich people who keep complaining that you're unhappy! Want to know how to be happy and fulfilled? Stop chasing the dragon of accumulation! Instead, work at making the lives of those around you better — especially your employees. They're giving you the hours that make up their lives after all. You'll be so much happier in the long run. Besides, titan of industry, Henry Ford said that it's your job:

"There is one rule for the industrialist and that is: Make the best quality of goods possible at the lowest cost possible, paying the highest wages possible."

A company doesn't just have a responsibility to make profits — it has a responsibility to distribute them fairly to the people who make those profits possible. By treating your employees well and compensating them as well as possible, you not only gain their loyalty but their appreciation as well. This, in turn, leads to higher levels of serotonin and oxytocin as you strengthen your workplace community.

THE DEATH OF MUTUAL AID

Greed, both for money and for power, is also shutting down one of humanity's most ancient and useful tools: mutual aid. This is exactly what it sounds like: groups and individuals working to help each other out with survival. Mutual aid is the original economic system,[40] and it has been the subject of an enormous amount of research.

Ambulance services began as mutual aid. After most large-scale disasters, the first relief efforts — the efforts of the community to help

---

40 Mutual aid is what helped primitive humanity to survive. See bibliography for more info.

45

each other — are mutual aid. Humanity is designed to help one another to survive, and we are quite effective at this. The fact that we've made it this far is a testament to our effectiveness. Mutual aid is direct and effective, and it's based on the concept of helping your neighbor. It's been around since before civilization, and even Jesus preached mutual aid in the "Corporal Works of Mercy." Clothing the poor, feeding the hungry, helping the sick, taking care of your neighbor — these are all forms of mutual aid.

The thing about mutual aid is that you can't really monetize it. In fact, it can decrease the profits of the wealthy — if ten families are willing to share and help one another, they may only need to buy five hammers instead of ten. They may be able to share two lawnmowers, instead of buying one per family. This sharing and communication draws communities closer and strengthens society but decreases profits for a handful of rich people. Not only that, but mutual aid weakens the hold of those in power by making people less dependent on them and more resilient as communities. When individuals will simply help each other, exploiting those in desperate situations becomes much harder — after all, if communities will help those in need, the needy don't have to go into debt just to survive.

Governments who wish to become authoritarian are also threatened by mutual aid because it means that the population doesn't have to rely solely upon them. If mutual aid groups that are providing valuable assistance become too large or popular, those in power might actually have to start serving the interests of the people as well or risk the rise of a political party who will.[41]

---

41 A few examples here are the International Worker's Order in the early 1900s, the Zapatista movement in Mexico in the 1990s, and the Black Panther Party's Free Breakfast for Children Program in the 1960s.

Regardless of the economic system, mutual aid is always an excellent goal to strive for. Communities becoming involved in taking care of each other makes us stronger and draws us together as a whole. We cannot disassemble our entire economic system and replace it with mutual aid, but pursuing it where possible will make communities — and through them the nation — more close-knit and better able to overcome hardship. Those who speak out against it may come up with all kinds of justifications, but ultimately, they do so because they don't want to see the American people working together to support each other. This is a big red flag, and like so much else, it's driven by greed for money and power.

CONTRIBUTIONISM: THE MIDDLE LINE

So. Communism? Not perfect. Socialism? Similar issues to communism.[42] Capitalism? Longer shelf life, but still not perfect. The common theme? Each is a "broad stroke" solution. They either say, "Everyone gets what the government says," or "Everyone takes what they can." We clearly need something more nuanced that combines the best parts of each.

Enter contributionism. As I addressed earlier, contributionism ties the earnings at the top of a company to the average earnings at the bottom of the company. It states that no leader of any company is allowed to earn more than ten times as much in an hour as their average entry-level employee. Again, let's remember what we discussed earlier — that time is the most precious commodity a person has, and that so long as they're each putting in effort, one person cannot do ten times more than another. It also introduces a certain amount of profit-sharing and places a cap on how much investors can earn by simply investing money.

Let's take a closer look at how economic contributionism works. For now, we'll take a broad look at the idea before getting into more nitty-gritty specifics later. So, if you have a question or concern, read on — it will likely be discussed in more depth later. We'll start by discussing wages.

---

42 This book isn't a comprehensive look at every economic system in history, so I mainly focused on capitalism and communism. Socialism — especially democratic socialism — is less extreme than communism but harbors many of the same problems: lack of incentives, government consolidation of power, and difficulties and inefficiencies in resource allocation.

INTERNAL COMPENSATION RATIOS — GREED MOTIVATING DECENCY

The beauty of contributionism is its realism. It *harnesses* the human desire to accumulate, rather than ignoring this drive. It does so by basing wages on a ratio rather than a hard cap, so the wages at the top are tied to the wages at the bottom. Like capitalism, this provides incentives for hard work — the more your company makes and the higher you rise, the more you can make yourself — but it also ensures that employers continue to compensate their workers fairly for the contribution of their time and effort, in keeping with the goals of Marxism.

In contributionism, companies are divided into "tiers." These serve as limits to how much a boss or manager can make compared to their employees. Each tier is a ratio, and entry-level employees make up Tier 1. A Tier 2 employee can make up to twice the average pay of an entry-level Tier 1 employee. A Tier 5 employee can make up to five times as much as Tier 1, and so on.

CONTRIBUTIONIST "TIERS"

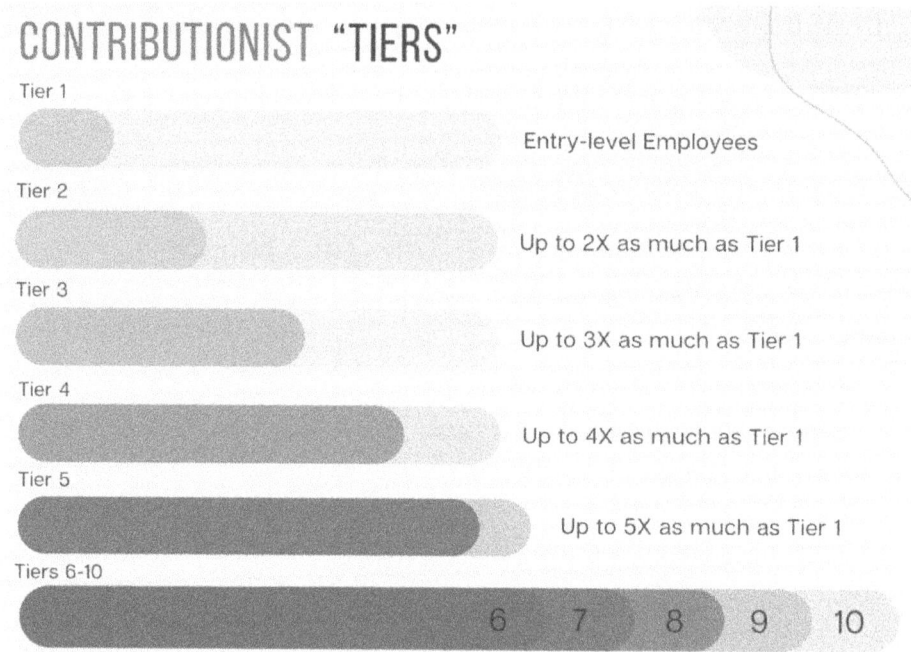

Tier 1
Entry-level Employees

Tier 2
Up to 2X as much as Tier 1

Tier 3
Up to 3X as much as Tier 1

Tier 4
Up to 4X as much as Tier 1

Tier 5
Up to 5X as much as Tier 1

Tiers 6-10
6   7   8   9   10

Each tier represents the maximum earnings compared to Tier 1.

The larger the company, the more tiers it can have, topping out with ten tiers for massive companies that have 10,000+ employees. At these mega-companies, the Tier 10 owner or CEO can earn up to ten times the hourly rate of their Tier 1 entry-level workers. We'll go into the individual tier breakdowns in more detail in the "Nitty-Gritty" section later. For now, it's enough to understand that the "tier" of an employee represents the limit of how much they can make compared to Tier 1, and that the ratio tops out at Tier 10 — ten times the entry rate.

By not placing a hard cap on earnings, employers can continue to make more and more money as their business grows — as long as they bring the people who make their success possible along with them. For instance, if you run a huge company in which you can pay entry-level employees $100,000 a year — and so on up the ladder — you yourself can make $1 million a year. If you do well and you're able to increase entry-level wages to $150,000 a year, you can be making $1.5 million a year. The sky's the limit. Beyond that, if you're putting in extra hours, you can earn extra money — the ten times cap is specifically on hourly earnings. Remember: hard work and long work are different things. Contributionism allows the extra hours to be recognized while still acknowledging the importance of the people making the company run.

Let's take just a moment to discuss why this is fair — why it's reasonable to say that employers don't need more than ten times greater income than their employees. Nowadays, we throw around massive numbers so much that they've lost all meaning. As I've mentioned, we know that in 2022 the average American CEO made *344 times more* than an entry-level employee, but we don't truly appreciate the scope and excess of that number. We've been conditioned to ignore it. So, let's take a quick second to appreciate what the path to *"just"* ten times income looks like in more concrete terms.

Let's say that you're paying an entry-level employee enough that they can buy a modest home and used car, take care of their bills, pay their medical expenses, go out to eat once a week, and go on a one-week vacation each year.

If you're making:	
2x	You own a nice, spacious house, drive a new car, eat at a nice restaurant each week, and go on two different vacations each year.
3x	You own a nice, spacious home as well as a modest vacation home. You drive a new car and go to a fancy restaurant each week. You go on two vacations a year and put a quarter of your employee's annual salary into your savings account each year.
5x	You own what your employee would call a mansion. You own a vacation home as well and drive a new luxury car. You go out to eat whenever you please, and you go on two vacations a year. You also put your entry-level employee's annual salary into your savings each year.
8x	All of 5x, but you also have a full-time housekeeper and a full-time personal assistant/driver, each paid the salary of your entry-level employee. You also put double your entry-level employee's salary into your savings each year.
10 x	You live in a mansion with a second, more modest home in another city. You also have a vacation home on a lake somewhere. You drive a fancy new car and go out to eat or drink whenever you like. You don't worry about basic living expenses or regular healthcare bills. You go on two vacations a year that are luxurious compared to your employee's vacation, and you put twice your employee's annual salary into your savings each year. You have a full-time assistant/driver and a full-time housekeeper for your mansion who each make your entry-level employee's annual salary.

My forward-thinking readers may be wondering about investors or people who own multiple companies. Fear not — we'll be covering those things more in the next section and in the "Loopholes" section toward the end. The quick answers are profit-sharing (sharing profits with employees, instead of giving them all to investors) and determining pay based on actual hours worked.

Now, while money doesn't buy happiness, it does translate to security and quality of life. To say, "I deserve ten times more pay than you" to an employee is to tell them "I deserve a quality of life ten times greater than yours because my time is ten times more valuable than yours."

Dear reader, consider how you would feel if someone were to say this to your face. If someone told you that your time — the moments that make up your life — is one-tenth as valuable as theirs. Really take a minute and consider that. This may seem like an extreme statement, but it reflects the mindset of upper management across the country and across the globe. In fact, it's a very *conservative* statement. Remember, the average ratio of CEO to worker compensation is *three hundred forty-four* to one, not ten to one. And remember, it's like this all the way down the ladder. If the CEO makes 344 times what you do, the next three beneath them likely make 300 times your pay. And the next ten down likely make 200 times your pay. And so on down the ladder, until we get to little old you — working a full, honest day for peanuts.[43]

---

43 Many CEOs sneak around this pay cap by paying themselves in company stock. For instance, Jeff Bezos only earned $81k in salary in 2022. This appears well within contributionist parameters. However, in 2024, Bezos sold off $13 *billion* in shares — his "realized income" was his salary, *plus* the value of his shares. The wealthy use stock value almost as a money laundering scheme, allowing them to hold billions of dollars in value while avoiding taxes and claiming they make very little money. It's a little like paying themselves in rare and valuable collectible trading cards, which they can then sell for actual

Contributionism's pay ratio policy is eminently fair. Consider also that the above example includes *one* earner. In the case of couples, both can be working jobs, increasing the total household income and means to a level far beyond what I've laid out here. I understand that this may not be enough of a "leveling of the playing field" for some, but it's FAR better than what we're seeing today, and it still provides a monetary incentive to work hard. On top of that, contributionism provides business owners with a direct incentive to pay their employees better — because more for their employees is how they get more for themselves.

It's also worth mentioning that this isn't a new concept. Similar things have not only been done, but they've also proven that they work extremely well. We'll get into that in the "Case studies" section later on with Ben & Jerry's, Patagonia, and more amazing examples of fair pay in action.

If you feel you still need more after receiving ten times as much as your entry-level employees, I've got some news for you: if you haven't found happiness and satisfaction yet, it isn't because you need more stuff — it's because your philosophy is broken. Spend some time reading different philosophical perspectives on living a good life and finding happiness. Your life will benefit far more from that than from a few more millions.

So, if we can be on board with the fact that you can live an *opulent* life on ten times an entry-level employee's income, let's take a look at the other main focus of contributionism: investment.

---

money. This is why we need compensation ratios both in salary *and* in profit-sharing. (See the next section: "ROI Caps.")

ROI CAPS – SALTING THE LEECHES

First, let's talk about how investment currently works. Again, this isn't a textbook, so this will be a "broad strokes" explanation. Say a company needs to raise funds either for startup or for expansion. In the current system, investors take a risk by purchasing shares in that company. These shares give them partial ownership of both the company and its profits. This ownership does not end until the company folds or the investor decides to sell their shares, either back to the company or to someone else. The investor continues to reap the rewards of the workers' labor — the profits that labor generates — forever, without ever setting foot on the company's property or doing a day's work for the company. This revenue motivates shareholders to pressure CEOs to continually increase profits so that they can pull in more money each year.

The problem is there's this thing in science called the "conservation of matter." Infinite growth is not possible within a closed system. Now, a new company has many areas in which it can increase profits. They can make better products, which they can then charge more for. They can find better deals on the materials required to make their products, lowering the cost of manufacturing and increasing net profit. They can take steps to streamline logistics to eliminate waste. They can invent or implement ways to manufacture more efficiently to turn out more product. They can increase marketing to find more buyers. They can replace incandescent light bulbs with LEDs to decrease operating costs.

A company that's been around for several decades has already implemented many of these changes. Yet shareholders in our current system continue to demand increasing profits; the first rule of corporate capitalism is that the profit number must go up. But the more streamlined a company has become, the more difficult it is to make profits increase further. It now takes extreme innovation, risky new ideas, and hard work

55

to come up with new ways to streamline a well-established business so that it becomes even more profitable.

Well, for the most part. If executives and investors are willing to throw ethics out the window, then there are several very easy, surefire ways that a company can ensure higher profits:

First, they can increase marketing. They can shove their product into people's faces as often as possible with different forms of advertising and work to convince those people that their life is missing something without it. This leads to overstimulation, dwindling attention span, and a loss of self-worth — but it does keep people buying, which increases profits.

Second, they can cut corners. They can do this on the quality of their products to save money, or by ignoring safety regulations for people and the environment. This leads to worse and worse products, the destruction of the environment, and health problems — but it does save money, which increases profits.

Third, they can lay off employees, cut benefits, stop raising wages, or ship manufacturing overseas to use close to slave labor in countries the consumer has never heard of. That leads to unemployment, widespread economic hardship, and a lower standard of living for millions — but it does save money, which increases profits.

SOUND LIKE A WORLD YOU'RE FAMILIAR WITH?

The issue with this system is that if investors continue to demand increasing profits, at some point, the only easy way to provide those profits is by making choices that cause harm to the Earth, society, or workers.

With our current system of "business owned forever by investors," workers are not seen as valuable parts of the company who are entitled to a share of the fruits of their labor — they're seen as an operating expense. Instead of being grateful to their workers for allowing their business to function and for making them money, investors and upper management see the people doing the actual work as an unfortunate cost. Something to try and trim back to increase their own profits. You don't need to be an ethicist to see that something is inherently wrong with treating the people doing the work as a cost to be minimized rather than as individuals giving the time that makes up their lives to facilitate your success.

Keep in mind, many investors will never do an ounce of work to actually make what the company is selling. They — or their parents — simply bought shares in the company and now make money from it for the rest of their lives, until the company goes down or they choose to sell. With enough shares, someone who has never worked a day in their life for a company can easily make more money from the workers' labor than the workers make themselves.[44]

Beyond that, this constant drain by investors hurts business. If a brilliant entrepreneur has a great idea for a company and needs to raise funds, they will forever be forced to pay a chunk of their profits to their investors unless they succeed in buying them out. This slows the growth of their business and limits the income of the business owner as well as

---

44 A few examples of this — using share prices in late 2024 and the dividend rates paid on those shares, here's how much it would cost to buy enough shares to generate $100k each year, without ever doing a day's work for the company. AT&T: just under $2 million. Coca-Cola: just over $3 million. Orchid Island Capital: just over $500k. Keep in mind, these shares are still owned by the investor. If the business doesn't tank, they can turn around and sell them and get their money back. Essentially, these investors are being paid $100k each year for "risking" their money in investment. But when you make $10 million a year (like many big CEOs) is that really a risk? Remember — when you have $100 million, you can give your children a $3 million stock portfolio for their eighteenth birthday that will generate them $100k a year without working, off the labor of others.

their workers. While investment is necessary to start many businesses, it can also hinder them in the long run and tends to lead to a frantic, even reckless, rush for profits.[45] We need a way to reward the valuable jump-start that investment provides while also allowing the business and the people who make it up to see the proper rewards of their labor.

Contributionism has a straightforward solution: it places a cap on ROI (return on investment). Based on the riskiness of the investment, the investor is automatically "bought out" when they hit a certain amount of earnings. For a low-risk investment, the upper limit of this cap is set at 100% — meaning that an investor is bought out when they've made their money back, plus 100% of what they put in, doubling their money. For a medium-risk investment, the cap's upper limit is set at 200% — an investor can triple their money. For a high-risk investment, it's set at 300%, allowing an investor to quadruple their money. In the case of each, businesses and investors can negotiate the actual amount, but the investor will be advised of the risk assessment and know the maximum they can receive going in. I'll discuss this more later, but keep in mind that even within our current system, the riskiness of an investment is assessed. This isn't a new concept — it already exists and simply needs to be applied within the contributionist model.

While the company has investors still being paid out, the investors are paid 50% of the company's profits. Of the remaining 50%, up to half goes to the company (for upgrades, financial padding, expansion, etc.) and the remainder is split between the employees and owner based on their tier and hours worked.

Once the investors are paid out, all of the profits are split, with up to 50% going back to the business, and the remainder (which must be at

---

45 "One of the most common ways VCs can inadvertently harm a company is by pushing for hyper-growth at any cost." See bibliography for articles with more details.

least 50%) is once again split between the employees and owner based on their tier and hours worked.

Considering that little actual direct work is being done by investors, these are very generous terms; give some money, and if all goes well, double it in a few years. Yes, there is, of course, the risk of losing that investment — something that employees don't need to worry about — but that's why the investor is entitled to doubling (or tripling or quadrupling) their investment without putting in any direct work. The employees are compensated for their time, and the investor is compensated for their risk — but there must be a cap to this risk compensation. To claim that taking a risk once entitles you to an eternal share in the profits is to claim that the risk you took is infinitely more valuable than the time of the workers who make the company run.[46] By capping investment returns, the value of workers' time and efforts is respected.

What's more, this approach facilitates growth for the business and increased profits for the people who make it work by eventually allowing all profits to be kept by them, once the investors have been "paid out." These profits can be used to build the business up more as well as increase both wages and the quality of goods. Of course, if the investor actually does work for the business, they can make their standard wages in addition to their investment earnings.

This system ensures that career investors continue finding new

---

46 If an investor invests $1 million, and after ten years they double their money, that risk was worth $1 million. But what if the company makes them another $1 million after five more years? Now the risk was worth $2 million. If another 20 years brings another $6 million, their risk was worth $8 million. Meanwhile, the workers' pay stays about the same and pays by the hour. The "value" of the investor's risk can potentially increase forever, while the value of the workers' time stays the same. To add insult to injury, this overvaluing of investor risk is one of the very things keeping the workers from seeing the full rewards of their work.

businesses to invest in and don't get to coast by without continuing to contribute to the growth of our nation. It's a system in which investors still have motivation to invest, while also spurring business growth and employee compensation by eventually releasing the business from the financial drain of its shareholders. It incentivizes investment in new businesses by ensuring that investors who want to make money must consistently be looking for new ventures to invest in and support. It's a compromise, allowing investors to still reap large rewards for their risk, while also maximizing resources for company growth and employee compensation.

Now, if you're onboard with the reasoning behind using a ratio for compensation and capping investment returns, we can start to really look at the benefits of contributionism.

THE BENEFITS OF CONTRIBUTIONISM

U nder contributionism, we aren't a country of government handouts — simply one that requires employees to be compensated fairly for their contribution of time and effort. This means no more people working a full-time job and still needing to supplement their income with food stamps or seek additional government support for childcare. Will government assistance still be necessary? For some, yes. But again: as of 2020, *70%* of people enrolled in Medicaid or food stamp programs worked full-time, according to research by the Government Accountability Office.[47] Higher wages upfront would mean a *huge* reduction in the need for government assistance, saving valuable tax dollars. As an extra bonus, the fact that working can actually get you somewhere again also means far greater motivation to seek a job in the first place — because jobs are much more tempting when they can actually help you get ahead. This means more people at work and fewer working people who need government aid.

FOR THE TAX RATE

By properly valuing work and diffusing wealth more fairly, the average income of the country's working class increases. This can allow lower, more simplified tax rates for all, including the wealthy. The reason that taxes on the wealthy are so high is that the rest of the country *doesn't have the money* to tax. As I've mentioned,[8] the bottom 50% of earners

---

47 The full report and key findings are available in the bibliography.

hold 2.5% of America's wealth. On the other side, the top 10% hold 70% of America's wealth — and they got there by not paying their workers fairly for their contribution.

Taxing the rich more isn't a matter of penalizing them; it's taking money out of the backend that should have been paid upfront because the working class doesn't have the money to afford to pay for the country's infrastructure for the rich. By making pay fairer on the frontend, the working class will have enough money to make tax rates fairer on the backend.

While we're on the subject of taxes, as an added benefit to having wealth more fairly distributed, contributionism means better resources for public schools and institutions like hospitals as well as emergency services. By distributing wealth more fairly based on contribution, you spread it out, meaning that the quality of public education and other services funded by taxes aren't as dependent on living in a wealthy area — the baseline of wealth of the nation has risen.

FOR THE QUALITY

Contributionism also allows the economy to function in the way capitalism is meant to in terms of market competition. By increasing wages, the average working citizen has more money — money that some may use to start their own businesses. This leads to an increase in competition between companies to turn out the best product possible. Unlike late-stage capitalism, which focuses on cutting corners to squeeze out every drop of profit possible, contributionism allows the free market to work as intended to promote high-quality goods and service.

FOR THE HOPE

There's also a less quantifiable benefit to the model of contributionism: hope. In psychology, there's a well-studied phenomenon called "learned helplessness." In a study with dogs, psychologist Martin Seligman sent small shocks into the dog's kennel through the floor.[48] Unable to get away, the dogs soon accepted the shocks as inevitable. Then, when Seligman reconfigured the floor so that only a portion delivered shocks, the conditioned dog simply lay on the electrified floor — not bothering to try and find an escape. The dogs had learned to accept the inevitable and gave up trying.

A similar effect can be observed in humans. By paying wages so low that they provide no hope of reaching a better situation, income inequality removes the desire to *try* to work for a better situation. On the other hand, if employment means fair pay and the ability to improve one's life, workers are far more motivated to seek out that employment.[49] This fact has been mentioned above, but it's worth pointing out that it has strong backing in psychology.

FOR THE SECURITY

This same "learned helplessness" also drives crime in poor communities. When you can't afford college, and most jobs you can get have no benefits and barely pay enough for food and rent, what is the

---

48 This study from the *Journal of Experimental Psychology* is available in the bibliography.

49 This is that whole "laissez faire" capitalism that right-wing elites tout. "If companies don't pay enough, nobody will work for them." Unfortunately, now that people are calling their bluff and demanding higher wages, states like Iowa have responded by lowering the age for factory work, and multiple states are practicing "convict leasing" — renting out prisoners as near-slave labor (paid between 3 cents an hour and $1.41 an hour depending on state). See bibliography for more.

appeal of an honest job? Scams, theft, and drug trafficking are much more lucrative. Sure, they're risky and morally questionable, but an honest job is a guarantee of poverty. It's also much easier to justify illegal actions when you have lacked opportunity.

When a person is born into a poor family, that wasn't their choice. When they go to an underfunded public school because they're in a poor neighborhood, that wasn't their choice. When their parents can't spend much time with them because they both work full-time jobs to provide food and housing, that wasn't the child's choice. So much is outside of their control, and they're aware of this unfairness. And — right or wrong — when we feel our situation is unfair, it's easy to justify bad actions as "balancing the scales." By providing a path to a good life through fair contribution for hard work, we keep the scales from needing to be re-balanced. Nothing will ever eliminate all crime, of course, but contributionism will make the nation safer by reducing the crimes committed out of desperation or necessity.

FOR THE KIDS

Another benefit of contributionism is what it does for our children's upbringing. Historically, single-parent homes have often been difficult places for children to grow up. This isn't for moral reasons — it's simply because children's formative years are meant to be spent with and guided by a parent. This can be a mother or a father, and throughout the mid-1900s, all the way up through the mid- '70s, one parent working while the other stayed home was more common than not.[50]

---

50 An average of 64% of families had one stay-at-home parent in 1967. By 2009, only an average of 34% of families could afford to do this. See bibliography for data.

This is due in large part to the fact that the single earner's income *allowed* them to do this. Compensation was fairer, and one parent's income could support a family. But, as business owners and investors have soaked up more and more of the profits from their workers' labor, a huge number of working-class families have become unable to support themselves on one person's income.[51] The result? Children of two-parent households now are in the same situation as children of one-parent households were in the past. With both parents working to support themselves and their child, they have less time to spend taking part in their child's development and supporting the efforts of teachers. That feeds back into the issues with our school system — one of teachers' biggest complaints nowadays is a lack of parental support.[52] Contributionism yields more quality time spent with kids, which leads to more well-developed and educated generations, which is how you build a better future.

FOR THE GRATITUDE

Another less quantifiable bonus from contributionism impacts employers and business owners specifically. If you make workers feel that their contribution is being acknowledged and rewarded by paying them appropriately, you get their loyalty, gratitude, and a better work ethic. If the owner of a company is limited to making ten times what their average entry-level employee is making, it benefits them to raise the pay of their employees. Knowing this, it benefits employees to be proactive in doing what they can to make more for the company — because the

---

51 This has a profound impact on our nation's children. See bibliography for more info and statistics.

52 A 2023 survey found that about 70% of teachers feel that parental involvement is insufficient. See bibliography for the survey.

more the company makes, the more the boss can pay them so that the boss, in turn, can make more themselves.

It's a system that combines the innate human desire to accumulate with ethical compensation in order to maximize motivation, productivity, and, incidentally, the gratitude and loyalty of employees to their employers for providing them a good job — not just a job that slows their slide into debt. It yields both a better quality of life and greater hope for employees, and a more fulfilling life for the employers who receive gratitude and appreciation for providing that quality of life.

FOR THE BALANCE

There's another bonus that will become apparent when I start getting into the nitty-gritty of how contributionism works. "Entry pay" must be at a certain minimum, which is determined based on the cost of living. This means that landlords gouging citizens on rent will directly increase the operating costs of companies — if the cost of living goes up, so does the minimum entry pay. This provides a check and balance between landlords and business, ensuring that even the bottom of the ladder is providing a decent quality of life for those putting in the hours.

FOR THE PLANET

Beyond all this, as money is diffused, private citizens can afford things like green energy upgrades. With investors eventually being "paid out," companies are likewise able to reinvest their profits in green and renewable energy infrastructure, ultimately lowering operating costs for employers and allowing the citizens of this country to live longer lives, free from the proven detrimental effects of pollution.[53] Moving toward this green energy infrastructure would also allow the U.S. to get closer to energy independence, enabling us to provide for our own needs and freeing us from relying on outside sources for fuel. What embodies "the land of the free" more than a nation of people who are no longer dependent on outside providers for energy needs?

FOR THE NATION

We live in a one-party system that gives us the illusion of choice. Both parties are in the pockets of big business, and they keep us at each other's throats so that we don't see the real problem. Campaign finance plays a huge role in this. By spending millions on campaign donations, companies have massive impacts on elections, essentially allowing the wealthy to buy political positions by funding massive marketing campaigns for their favored candidate. With contributionism's profit-sharing, and the fact that it doesn't count political donations as an "expense" (which we'll talk about in the "Nitty-Gritty" section), the amount that companies have to spend to influence elections is reduced, allowing our democracy to function more as it was designed.

---

53 Whether you believe in climate change or not, *pollution* is a massive problem in itself. Beyond damage to our ecosystem, the pollution of soil, water, and air leads to a terrifying array of negative health impacts for us as individuals. See bibliography for a more detailed breakdown of each.

TO SUMMARIZE

Under contributionism, communities gain wealth, and the population as a whole becomes stronger, making our nation stronger as well. This increased wealth leads to:

- Greater ability to afford healthcare.
- An increase in hope of improving your situation.
- An increase in motivation to work.
- A decrease in negative behaviors associated with poverty, such as theft, murder, and drug or alcohol addiction, and a decrease in (understandable) classism as a result of these behaviors.
- Better educational opportunities.
- Greater parental involvement in child-raising.
- Better products as more small businesses bring market competition.
- Better distribution of government services based on tax zones.
- More fulfilled employers and business owners, who receive their workers' gratitude and a motivated workforce.
- A sustainable world that's healthier and more beautiful to live in.
- A better quality of life for the vast majority of citizens.

Call me old-fashioned, but Boy Scouts taught me to leave every place better than I found it. These benefits would combine to make the world a better place for all, not just financially but also mentally, emotionally, and physically. It is the rising tide that lifts all ships, even while it preserves the capitalist motivation to work hard for a better life.

I can't stress this enough: this isn't a new system. It's several tweaks on the current one. The "money in and money out" doesn't need to be changed, just reshuffled and distributed more ethically and fairly. We CAN do this without tearing down and rebuilding the whole system. Pay policies similar to what I hope to formalize with contributionism are what ushered in an American golden age. Any excuses about complexity or impracticality are just that — excuses. Go watch stock traders shuffle numbers around to make fortunes and tell me what we have right now isn't overly complex.[54] Watch them make a mistake and lose six thousand people's retirement funds and tell me that the system we have currently isn't impractical.[55]

---

[54] For-profit market manipulation is rampant these days and has led to several economic crises. See bibliography for more info on what it is, as well as examples.

[55] For a scholarly article by the Urban Institute on how stock trading impacts retirements, see bibliography.

A SECTION FOR MY WEALTHY READERS

I'm sure that there will be members of the wealthy class who read this. I certainly hope there are — because we really do need you, too. Wealthy or poor, you're just as much a victim of history as everyone else is. Nobody chooses the society that they're born into or the historical circumstances that shaped it — we're simply the current baton holders in a relay race that goes back 2000 generations.[56] "Society" is just the product of a series of wild hand-offs by scared, short-lived creatures doing their best to survive in the world they live in. The society we were handed isn't one that's designed to bring happiness — it's designed to make and sell products. Beyond that, technology and the environment are changing the world we live in faster than ever before — which means that the information we have been handed in the "baton pass" from past generations is less representative of the needs of the present. Rich or poor, we have all been shaped by this.

I also want to recognize the fact that many of you got where you are today through hard work and determination and that these attributes should be rewarded. All the hours of overtime, the financial risk, the stress of piloting a business to success — what was the point of any of it if you wind up with the same as everyone else?

There's a common saying: "Everything in moderation." Chocolate is great, but eat too much and you run into health problems. Contributionism is a form of moderation within business. If communism says, "Don't eat chocolate," and capitalism says, "Eat all the chocolate

---

56 Estimates vary and go as high as 9,294 generations, so I feel that my "2000" estimate is fair. See bibliography for more.

you can get your hands on," contributionism is saying, "Eat some chocolate, but make sure you share it with the people who helped you get it." Finding this moderation will not only make the world you live in better, but it will also directly improve your life as well.

I'm not pitching some sort of utopia where there's no crime and everyone is happy all the time. Idealism is all well and good, but without realism to ground it, it can create as many problems as it solves. If we're looking at things from a realistic perspective, there are three big reasons why contributionism is a good idea for the wealthy: avoiding problems, gaining peace of mind, and being a pioneer.

AVOIDANCE

Let's start with avoidance. If you're profiting tens of millions of dollars while workers are making next to minimum wage — especially if you're just a shareholder — there's something wrong here. This is *wrong* — and, as the bible says, we reap what we sow. By doing wrong to society, we do it harm. We make it worse, not just for others, but also for ourselves. It may impact the poor first, but as part of society, the lives of the wealthy eventually get worse too. And all too often, they get *much* worse.

They say that the historian's curse is to be doomed to watch people repeat the mistakes of the past. Well, one of the cycles that rules humanity is the cycle of wealth. History is full of dynasties, kingdoms, and empires that have fallen when the disparity in wealth became too great — when the people at the top enriched themselves too much at the expense of those at the bottom. One of my personal favorite examples of this was when, in *ancient* (and sometimes debated) Chinese history, the Xia dynasty was toppled after the ruling family made a lake of wine, they could sail boats on. This was a bit too much for the starving masses of China, and they violently overthrew their rulers. After the fighting died

71

down, the Shang dynasty took over (which is not debated). They ruled for several hundred years, consolidating wealth until — guess what? — they decided to make their own wine lake. From there, it didn't take long for the dynasty to come crashing down. Two multi-century dynasties, back-to-back, both toppled when they reached the same level of greed.[57]

This may be my favorite example, but it's far from the only one. History is littered with them — the Bourbons of France, the Romanovs of Russia, the decline of Rome — but the cycle keeps repeating because people fail to learn from it. And every time the cycle happens, it leads to ugly results. The situation becomes intolerable for the majority of society, violence breaks out, the country is thrown into chaos, and ultimately those in power — who thought they were untouchable — suddenly find themselves receiving a free neck adjustment from Dr. Guillotine.

At the moment, we're still living in a world where many people see a CEO get shot and say, "Violence is never the answer." This line of thinking, this "_____ is never alright" mentality, is representative of deontology, an ethical framework developed by Immanuel Kant.[58] "Lying is always wrong," "stealing is always bad," etc. Deontology is a set of lovely, simple rules that work best in a good, uncomplicated world.

---

57 If you're a history nerd, see bibliography for more info on these dynasties.

58 Kant's quote expressing this comes from his concept of a moral imperative, which he sums up as: "Act only according to that maxim whereby you can at the same time will that it should become a universal law." To translate: "Don't do something unless you hope that everyone else will do it too." As a practical example, this would mean one should never tell a lie because if everyone lied about everything, the world would be a bad place. Like I said: nice and simple — perfect for kindergarteners.

But as soon as things start getting complex, it becomes apparent that pure deontology is ethics for children.[59]

There is a famous thought experiment against Kantian ethics called "The Murderer at the Door." Imagine your friend comes to your house in a panic, saying a murderer is chasing them and asking you to hide them. You do so. A few moments later, there is a knock on the door. You open it to see a man holding a knife. He tells you he intends to kill your friend and asks you where they are. Do you tell him? According to Kant's deontology, a lie is wrong, so the ethical thing to do is to tell the truth and give up your friend to be murdered. Even if you have some means of defense like a firearm, you can't use it because, according to deontology, killing is also wrong.

My point in this mini philosophy lesson is this: deontology does not do well in moral gray areas. And the harder things get for people — the more you squeeze them — the grayer morality becomes. When the people wise up and realize who the murderer at their door really is… Do you think they're going to keep choosing to let the murderer have what they want? What would you choose? When people realize that wealthy corporations (and those responsible for their actions) are to blame for their hardships but that they're shielding themselves from all repercussions with laws that they bought and paid for — do you really think that the people of this nation will continue to say, "violence is *never* the answer?" Sooner or later, their sense of ethics will mature, and they'll begin to see shades of gray.

Please don't misunderstand me — this isn't a threat. It's a plea. We can avoid all this if we simply do what so many before us have failed to do: set aside our arrogance and have the humility to actually *learn* from

---

59 A comprehensive article on this subject and the shortcomings of pure deontology can be found in the Stanford Encyclopedia of Philosophy. More info and citation in the bibliography.

the past. In this case, the lesson history teaches us is that it's in the wealthy's own best interest to treat people fairly rather than soaking up all the profits of their workers' efforts. Perhaps asking people to learn from the past is too ambitious a request — after all, it doesn't happen often — but a fella's gotta try.

PEACE OF MIND

Avoiding the "destruction" part of the cycle of history is all well and good, and what the wealthy stand to gain is related: peace of mind. Peace of mind is a wonderful thing — and one that is highly underrated. But the term gets thrown around a lot without being formally defined. What exactly *is* peace of mind? It's the absence of mental unrest. Unrest isn't just fear — it can be all sorts of things: stress, worry, uncertainty, guilt; they're all forms of mental unrest that prevent us from having peace of mind.

As wealth within a society consolidates, unrest grows. For the poor, it comes from economic stress, uncertainty, and hopelessness. As this consolidation continues and the many get poorer while the few get richer, more and more people become willing to turn to crime — especially against the wealthy. I can't imagine it's fun to worry each night that your house may be robbed or having to hire security to go places. I can't imagine it's enjoyable to see the hatred of so many fellow citizens directed at you. These potential threats damage our peace of mind — and through it, both our mental and physical health.[60] With contributionism, sure, you may not have as much money. But you can still have an awful

---

60 Isolation, paranoia, and a distorted sense of purpose are just a few things therapists are encountering in the wealthy. See bibliography for more info on this, as well as on the physiological impacts of stress.

lot of it if you work hard, and the peace of mind you get will help you to enjoy the experience of life more.

Many wealthy readers may resist this. They may worry that they won't be able to afford their lifestyle if they make less money. In fact, according to a 2024 study done by PYMNTS, 36% of individuals making $200k or more are living paycheck to paycheck.[61] This must be a terribly stressful situation, and it brings me to one of my favorite quotes: Gandhi's "live simply so others may simply live." There is certainly wisdom in this, but it goes deeper than altruism and caring for others. Just "living simply" is a massive gift to yourself. When you live simply — when you live beneath your means — you gain peace of mind and freedom from worry. If you're earning $200k each year and spending all of it on fancy cars, homes, and dinners, then losing your pay can mean bankruptcy, eviction, and repossession. What an awful weight to be carrying around! But what if you live beneath your means? If you make $200k and you live on a $100k budget, a surprise bill isn't a concern. If you lose your job, you likely have several years of savings to fall back on. You're free from the worries of need and scarcity. You're not trapped in your job because losing it won't be much more than a bump in the road — meaning that you have the freedom to leave if your employer treats you poorly or asks you to do something unethical.

If you're in the top 10% of earners, there isn't really an excuse for living paycheck to paycheck — but there is a reason: peace of mind is consumerism's biggest enemy. Peace of mind means contentment, and people who are content don't tend to be as driven to buy more things. But if you can convince people that their lives are missing something, it's much easier to get them to buy your product or service. As I've said

---

61 For people earning $100k and up it's even worse — with 48% of earners living paycheck to paycheck. See bibliography for more details.

before, none of us chose to be born into the consumerist society that we live in. Nonetheless, we have all been immersed in its mental conditioning, making us less content with our lives so that we'll buy more things. The way around this is realizing that this drive to consume more and more is just a marketing trick that has been deeply ingrained within our psyche. Freedom from financial worry will do a lot more for your happiness in the long run than buying a yacht.

The pursuit of profits above all else, with its constant need to influence politics and the minds of masses, takes an enormous amount of energy and resources. It's like swimming against a powerful current just to reach a location that isn't any better than the water downstream. Contributionism, and a reduced need for profits, gets rid of all this effort, and allows society to simply function, becoming far more stable than it is when people are wrestling for control.

PIONEERS

So, contributionism will help you to avoid the ugly part of the historical cycle of wealth inequality. It will help you to obtain greater peace of mind, allowing you to enjoy life more. This brings me to the final part, which is the opportunity to be a pioneer. As I've mentioned, we are simply the most recent links in the chain of humanity. For most of human history, our ancestors were at the mercy of the environment, and our society is the result of hundreds of generations reacting to the events around them as they tried to survive in a difficult and uncertain world. Even political conflicts like wars are the result of this, with countries angling for the resources that different regions bring.

However, over the last 150 years, this has changed. For the first time in human history, we control the environment more than it controls us.[62] Instead of simply reacting to hardships as they occur, we now have the luxury of being proactive. In the information age, we have the data we need to make informed decisions and deliberately craft a better world.

This is our opportunity to be pioneers. Imagine that two scientists with no knowledge of each other make the same discovery. If one of these scientists finishes their work a month before the other, they will be praised as a genius and immortalized in scientific history. The other scientist will be forgotten. Is this second scientist's discovery any less impressive? They did the same work as the first and found the same answer independently, yet people are unimpressed. The only difference between the two is novelty. I don't know how to do calculus. I'm not too proud to admit that. If I went off to the woods and lived in a cabin for six months and invented calculus on my own, would anybody care? Of course not. It's already been done. Being the first to do something is what enshrines your name in the halls of history. Contributionism is a chance to do something new. Something that will increase the quality of life for everyone — both the poor *and* the rich. If the wealthy are willing to give contributionism a go, they will be pioneers of a better world. Humans throughout time have sought some form of immortality — why not claim this by pioneering a new way and shepherding in a new era?

THE RISING TIDE LIFTS YOU, TOO

Beyond all this—and I can't stress this enough—improving the lives of those working for you improves your quality of life as well. As more Companies pursue Contributionism, more workers throughout the

---

62 Scientists have a word for this: *anthropogenic*. See bibliography for a full article on the subject.

country live better lives. Yes, you may no longer have hundreds of times as much as them, but the fact that you're living in a country filled with people who are happier and less desperate will mean that your base level of happiness will be higher.

In our current situation, you essentially have millions of tickets in a rickety, independent amusement park full of unhappy people with no tickets. Wouldn't you enjoy yourself more if you still had plenty of tickets for rides, but you were in a beautiful destination theme park along with many other happy people?

CASE STUDIES

Now, I think it's time for a few practical examples. Contributionism isn't some idealistic dream — similar structures have already been employed by several successful modern companies to great effect. These include Ben & Jerry's, W. L. Gore & Associates, Patagonia, and Gravity Payments. Some details on each:

BEN & JERRY'S

Ben and Jerry's is a name that is almost synonymous with "ice cream" in the U.S. They were also a contributionist all-star, with a longstanding company policy that the highest-paid employee should make no more than five times as much as the lowest-paid employee. Not only that, but they historically offered profit-sharing to employees as well. While things have shifted back to standard corporate profiteering after their acquisition by Unilever, their initial pay policies are what allowed them to become such a powerhouse in their field.

- After implementing their 5-to-1 pay ratio policy in 1985, the company experienced significant growth, expanding from a single ice cream shop to a major international brand.
- From 1990 to 1999, before their acquisition by Unilever, Ben & Jerry's saw steady growth, with revenues increasing from $77 million to $237 million — a roughly 308% growth over nine years. This equates to an average annual growth rate of approximately 20%.[63a]
- It should be noted that Ben & Jerry's pay ratio was raised toward the end of the '90s. This was due to the fact that CEO Ben Cohen

---

63 See bibliography for sources.

was retiring, and the company was unable to find a CEO who was willing to accept the 5-1 pay ratio.[63b] This isn't a black mark against pay ratios — it's a symptom of the greed of the business class.

W. L. GORE & ASSOCIATES

This company may not sound familiar to everyone, but their product, Gore-Tex fabric, is beloved by outdoor enthusiasts and military surplus lovers everywhere. This company caps the highest-earning employee at 20 times the lowest-earning employee. This may be more than contributionism proposes, but it's far better than the ratios in the three hundred-to-one range that we usually see. Beyond that, they also offer profit-sharing.

- W. L. Gore has been listed on Fortune's "100 Best Companies to Work For" list for 22 consecutive years (as of 2021).[64a]
- The company reported revenues of $4.8 billion in 2021, showing steady growth over the years.[64b]
- Their employee retention rate is notably high, with a turnover rate of 3% compared to the industry average of 14%. Low turnover significantly reduces hiring and training costs.[64c]
- W. L. Gore has over 3,000 patents worldwide, indicating high productivity and innovation from experienced, motivated workers.[64d]

PATAGONIA

Patagonia is one of the biggest names in outdoor apparel and gear. They haven't made their profit ratios public, but they are known to have relatively equitable pay practices, and they offer employee profit-

---

64 See bibliography for sources.

sharing. This has boosted employee retention and work ethic, helping them to boost profits even as they provide a good quality of life for their employees.

- The company has seen consistent growth, with sales increasing from about $20 million in 1990 to over $1 billion in recent years.[65a]
- Patagonia reports an employee turnover rate of 4%, significantly lower than the national average of around 57%.[65b]
- The company consistently ranks high on "Best Places to Work" lists, which can lead to reduced recruitment costs and higher productivity.

These are three heavy-hitting companies that have achieved massive success within their industry. None of them have been slowed down by paying executives less so they can pay workers more. None have been slowed down by sharing profits with their workers. In fact, their success is due in part to the loyalty that this pay provides. Loyalty doesn't just mean better work ethic — it also means less turnover, which means more experienced employees. As these companies grow and expand, it means more money for everyone involved — CEOs included.

GRAVITY PAYMENTS

One final example: Gravity Payments. Gravity Payments is a credit card processing company based out of Seattle, Washington, which received considerable attention relatively recently. The company made headlines in 2015 when it raised the minimum pay for workers to $70k

---

65 See bibliography for sources.

per year, in some cases doubling employees' pay. To do this, the founder, Dan Price, took a $1 million pay cut, ultimately receiving similar pay to his employees. He was ridiculed by many wealthy elites as being "anti-capitalist" and a socialist. Rush Limbaugh said that Gravity Payments would be "a case study in MBA programs on how socialism does not work, because it's gonna fail".[66] In actuality, they have since doubled employees, tripled business, and employee home-buying has gone up by ten times. While Dan himself is a problematic figure,[67] his ideas around compensation are sound. The results of Gravity Payments' compensation policies show that paying well isn't just possible — it can help companies blossom.

This concept I'm trying to codify with contributionism doesn't just work — it works well. It drives up productivity, increases innovation, leads to better lives for workers, and enables hard work and entrepreneurship to pay off. The only thing contributionism isn't good at is making a small handful of people at the top unimaginably rich, while keeping workers poor and desperate.

I can't emphasize it enough — this is not an entirely new system. It's an adjustment to the current one. There are examples today of companies thriving under policies that echo contributionism. Wealthy elites and their various political and media mouthpieces WILL make excuses about why it won't work, but do not let them fool you — there is no reason

---

66 In 2018, Harvard Business School released an article about Gravity Payments entitled, "Three years ago, this boss set a $70,000 minimum wage for his employees—and the move is still paying off." See bibliography for this article and Rush Limbaugh's original comment.

67 Dan has been accused by multiple women of sexual misconduct. While this is inexcusable, it doesn't change the effect his policies had upon his employees or the business.

why contributionism can't be put into effect in a widespread capacity, either through legislation or consumer pressure.

WHERE TO GO FROM HERE?

I f, at this point, contributionism sounds like a great concept to you — awesome! We're in agreement. So, what do we do now? Though contributionism will lead to a better experience of life and greater happiness for all, rich and poor, many of the wealthy in our own time and throughout history have proven to be stubbornly short-sighted and self-interested.

It's important to remember that there will be people who oppose contributionism. They will come out of the woodwork, calling it socialism or communism or impossible idealism. They'll say it's too complex or that it will hurt the economy or any number of excuses. They'll try to find a way to convince people that contributionism can't or shouldn't happen. The reason is simple: working Americans far outnumber the "leisure class." The only way they can keep siphoning off money from the labor of their workers is if they can keep us divided and distracted.

When the excuses do come, you need to remember that they're just that. Excuses. As we just discussed, there are plenty of actual case studies calling B.S.. The people making these excuses are doing so out of self-interest driven by *greed*, not the well-being of our nation. They aren't opposing contributionism just because they want to be wealthy — remember, contributionism does allow for wealthy individuals and an upper class. They're opposing it because they want to be unfathomably wealthy (a person who makes $1 billion per year makes $8k *every minute* they work) and they don't mind if that means the people who make it possible for them have to struggle.

We might just have to make a better world for everyone in spite of them.

There are a couple of ways we can do this: independently through the market or through legislation. For best results, we should pursue both.

THE DIRECT ROUTE: THE FREE MARKET

The quickest and most direct choice is to work through the market and through public solidarity. I break this down in much more detail in the "What Can I Do?" section on page 115, but I do want to mention it here before diving into the Nitty-Gritty details of how contributionism works. I recognize that for some readers, the ins and outs of an economic system might be a bit of a slog. I don't want to lose anyone before getting to the actionable stuff, so if you're already sold, or if you feel yourself losing interest in all the little details, don't give up! Just jump ahead to "What Can I Do?"

The direct approach can look a lot like Occupy Wall Street, but this time, there's a clear "ask": insisting that employers be transparent with pay and follow contributionist pay structures.

If companies refuse to do so, the contributionist movement should immediately boycott their goods, and their workers should find new jobs as soon they're able — or leave together to start their own business. After all, collectively they have the skills to make a business run — they just need to figure out their supply chain, find a knowledgeable person to hire as a consultant, and pool some money or find a loan to get it off the ground.

All of this doesn't necessarily have to happen overnight, but as people leave their companies, a good number may start new ones of their own that operate according to the contributionist model. Support them. Give them your business. Even if it means planning a few more minutes for your drive or paying a couple dollars more — help them to succeed. This will open up new jobs for others who are trying to leave the current model, providing workers with more options and increasing pressure on non-contributionist companies. At the same time, more products being created by contributionist companies means more opportunities for consumers to buy from those companies instead of non-contributionist establishments, further increasing the pressure.

At the end of the day, our problem must be dealt with the way greed is always dealt with: by altering the math so it's in the company's best interests to change. They may not always do the right thing morally, but you can count on them to do the financially sound thing. If their choice is "make less" or "make nothing," most will choose the former. Even if politics doesn't lead to a change, this on its own can force one.

Left or right, most of us can agree that the government as it currently stands is owned by business interests and lobbying groups. They won't all fight for us — so we must fight for ourselves. The way to do that is through supporting one another and using the free market. Could this make life a little less convenient for us for a while? Sure, but compare that inconvenience to the challenges that humanity has faced in the past. All of us have ancestors who faced down extreme, life-threatening adversity so that we could exist today. Surely, we can face the adversity of doing a little research and supporting contributionist businesses. Surely, we can have the fortitude to wait a couple of extra days for something to ship or to pay a few extra dollars to buy from good companies. If we can't even do that, how can our ancestors look at us with anything but disappointment?

All of this means actively supporting your community and other working people. Leaving your job or insisting on higher pay is a risky thing to do, especially now that companies have maneuvered us so that many folks are living from paycheck to paycheck. We must have

Remember: it may seem difficult now. People are living hand to mouth and struggling for economic stability. But it will only get harder. Fifteen years ago, people were in a much more stable place than they are today. Fifteen years from now, we'll be looking back at how much more stable things were today. The more we delay, the more businesses will push us into living on the edge of desperation and the harder it will be to push for change.

community and support in real life — not just on social media. Check in with your friends, work to strengthen your community, and if someone is out of a job, help them out if you're able. Provide emotional support. Help them to start new endeavors. It's a lot easier to stay strong when your community has your back. In coming together as communities, not only will we help to facilitate change, but we'll also be regaining something that has been taken from us by the modern world.

THE RISE OF THE MACHINES

A side from being forced into deeper and deeper desperation, there's another big problem that comes with delayed action: the rise of automation. Many companies' knee-jerk reaction will be to attempt to use AI technology to automate jobs as people leave, instead of the bosses simply taking a pay cut to pay them fairly.

It's also worth noting that the more sociopathic among the wealthy are counting down the days until they can automate foundational jobs like farming, logistics, and infrastructural upkeep. At the same time, certain elements in politics are trying to do away with agencies aimed at protecting American citizens, like the FDA and the EPA. That means removing protections that keep the bottom 75% of earners from getting poisoned by business — all while the cost of healthcare skyrockets.

The mega-wealthy will, of course, be immune to this since they can afford private farms and manors (or nations, in the case of Greenland) in favorable areas to escape most of the harmful effects of business-related pollution. They can easily afford cutting-edge medical treatments and preventative care. To anyone paying attention, this should be a bit spooky; we're seeing the wealthy working to develop technology to replace farmers, truck drivers, and other blue-collar workers with machines, while at the same time, they're trying to do away with regulations that keep the non-rich from being poisoned by pollution. I know that the wealthy are not stupid. If I were more conspiracy-minded, I'd call this a setup for slow-moving classicide. One that is slow enough to not raise alarm but fast enough to eliminate the non-rich as they're no longer required to provide for the wealthy.

Perhaps that's too cynical. Perhaps it's simply the result of many different rich people blindly chasing profits, consequences be damned. Either way, the society in which we live is changing faster than it ever has before. With the coming of AI and robotics, our very relationship to labor is undergoing a change never before seen in human history.

Throughout history, people have been needed to do different jobs to benefit the community. We came up with money so that people could have a way of exchanging the value of their work indirectly. We needed a wide variety of jobs, so there was a job for everyone. But what happens as more and more farms automate? What happens when accounting takes a tenth of the number of employees? Or as more and more customer service is done by bots? What happens when freight is handled by fully AI warehouses and trucks? Or when fishing ships get automated?

Even if everyone doesn't lose their job, what happens when each field requires a fourth of the workers? Will prices just drop as automation replaces jobs and reduces payroll? Think about all the stores with obnoxious self-checkouts — have your grocery prices gone down? Or have the owners' profits simply gone up?

Contributionist movement or not, we're headed for massive layoffs as companies try to cut jobs to increase profits for the shareholders and CEOs. This means that boycotting goods is especially important now and that it will become more important as we progress into the future. If enough people stop buying products from companies that have used automation for mass layoffs, those companies are left with a building full of expensive machinery and no money coming in from sales.

89

In our society, we vote with our wallets — we must vote against companies using AI to lay off workers. Otherwise, the jobs will dry up, and politicians in the pockets of big business will just keep finding new scapegoats to keep us distracted. Yes, the use of AI may decrease the cost of goods, but when your income is $0 because 90% of jobs have gone to robots, how many goods can you actually buy? Even if a new coffee maker costs $3 because it's made by robots, that's $3 more than you have, because robots have taken your job.

Apologists for the elites may point out that we always lose jobs during an industrial revolution. But with the coming of AI and the ability to mass automate, people stand to lose jobs more rapidly than ever before — with a projected 73 million U.S. jobs lost to automation by the year 2030.[68] As of December 2024, the civilian labor force was estimated at around 168.5 million people. 73 million jobs lost means more than a third of the country out of work. Politicians funded by the wealthy may blame things like immigration for the lack of jobs, but in doing so, they reveal who they're truly working for. If they honestly cared about jobs, they would be focused on corralling automation and AI, not diverting public attention to another issue that isn't the main cause of the problem.

The looming threat of mass job replacement is also an excellent reason to consider some form of Universal Basic Income, funded by charging a tax for automated jobs, which is lower than what the pay rate of that job would be for a human worker. It's a route that would still increase employer profits but would also generate

---

68 We have already lost millions of jobs to AI in the U.S. alone. See bibliography for more details.

a large amount of money that could be pooled and split by those out of work. I'll explain this strategy in more detail in the "Loopholes" section.

THE LONG-TERM ROUTE: LEGISLATION

The best way to ensure long-term success is through legislative change, especially when it comes to the investment side of things. In the America that we live in now, this poses challenges. Our politicians rely on the hyper-wealthy for campaign funds, which means they must serve the interests of the hyper-wealthy to get elected and re-elected. To overcome this, we must petition officials to support contributionism and make it clear to them that not supporting it will have a bigger negative impact on their poll results than the loss of advertising dollars. We may not be able to make politicians altruists, but if we can change the math to make it more worthwhile to do the right thing, we can make it in their own interests to work for the people.

Something that will help immensely is voting reform. I won't go into it too deeply because this is about contributionism, not voting reform. But in order to foster any progress, contributionism or otherwise, we *must* fix the voting system. The way it currently stands, all the two parties have to do is whip up enough fear of the other to make sure everyone votes for them. This is why every year is "the most important election ever." The more each party can stir up fear about the other, the less they have to do and the more they can get away with. Of course, things have become corrupt — we keep having to choose the lesser of two evils.

The problem is, if you keep choosing the lesser evil, you're still choosing evil. It's no wonder our situation has degenerated the way it has. Again, regardless of the side you're on, voting reform helps you.

Ranked Choice Voting[69] is a system with excellent promise for getting rid of the two-party system that our founders warned us about. Please look into it and advocate for it, because it doesn't just serve the left or the right — it serves the people as a whole.

FINAL NOTE BEFORE BRASS TACKS

One more philosophical note: notice that the system I set out below is intended to prevent abuse and exploitation. Some of the more greedy or lazy people — or those more deeply programmed by our cult of consumerism — will inevitably try to find loopholes. Those people are missing the point of the system and, fundamentally, the point of existence: we find true fulfillment from strengthening our pack. It's easy to forget with today's global business model that your pack includes the people who work for you.

Consumerist culture provides happiness that is easy, fleeting, and low quality. By chasing fortunes greater than hundreds or thousands of families' income, you're chasing the wrong thing. The trope of the unsatisfied rich person is common, and yet people don't seem to take in the lesson. Sure, be comfortable. Be secure. Have fun experiences. But don't forget about the people who are giving the moments that make up their lives to make it possible for you. Aim to raise the tide for all ships.

---

69 If you look at one item in the bibliography, please look at this one. We NEED a way to get out of this two-party system. Our founders warned us about this, and right now, we're seeing why. Advocate for it, both to your friends and your political representatives. In the U.S., political representatives and their contact info can all be easily found at both congress.gov and house.gov. Reaching out can truly take fifteen minutes.

THE NITTY-GRITTY

INTRO

S
o far, we've discussed why contributionism is an excellent balance between capitalist productivity and communist ethics. We've discussed how it can lead to a higher average quality of life for all workers, while still providing incentives for hard work. How it can increase the motivation of the workforce and the broader population. How it can foster more market competition to ensure the best products and services possible. How it can lower overall tax rates and boost education and public services. How it can facilitate the growth of business by eventually eliminating the profit drain of shareholders. Now, we'll get into more specifics of how I propose contributionism should work.

What you've read up to this point is all you need to know for a general understanding of contributionism. As the title suggests, this section is all about the nitty-gritty details that make it work. If you're just looking to understand the basic theory, you've read all you need. Stop now. Take a rest. Consider yourself informed. If you're more detail-oriented and you want specifics, do read on. I've included this section because I find that the difference between theory and practice is often specificity, and I'd like to answer as many questions as possible before they're asked.

Keep in mind that I'm a philosopher, not a CEO. When being put into practice, it is possible to make some tweaks. If I say that a company can have five tiers once they employ at least 100 people, this number may need slight adjustment. The focus of this book is on how a business should treat the people who make it successful. We are looking at business from the perspective of ethics and morality — because business without ethics is how you turn lives into nightmares. Type "Congolese

93

child hand" into Google Images, if you need any persuading on that point. Or check the bibliography, where I've provided it for you, as well as more information.[70] And the thing is, people living in a nightmare usually kill the ones inflicting it on them. This isn't a threat — it's history. Just ask King Louis XVI.[71] It's in everyone's best interest to grow up and at least pretend that we can learn from the past.

I understand that switching over to a new, improved system may be tricky. But as I've mentioned, contributionism doesn't seek to totally overhaul our economic system, instead seeking to preserve the best parts of capitalism while minimizing its abuses. We put humans on the moon. We intend to put them on Mars. Surely, we can tweak our pay structure so that workers are compensated fairly.

Keep in mind, I've tried to be thorough enough here to guide legislative policy. For a grassroots movement, it may be difficult to enact all of this at once. That's okay. In the beginning, we can simply push for pay transparency and ratio pay. The rest can come later. But it's hard to get to a destination without a complete map, so I've laid it all out here. Use the parts that you can at the moment, and push for the others as you're able.

All that said, here's how it would work.

---

70 See bibliography for an article on the effects of Belgian corporations in the Republic of the Congo, as well as a horrifying picture of the results of unrestricted enterprise. Be warned: it's disturbing.

71 King Louis XVI was publicly executed by guillotine during the French Revolution. He had prepared a final speech, which was cut short by a drumroll — he had angered people enough that they really weren't much interested in what he had to say.

REGARDING BUSINESS AS A WHOLE

Business, in general, can continue to function much the same as it has. In our current system, when a company decides upon pay rates, "payroll" is one item on the "cost side" of the budget, along with material costs, operating costs, marketing, etc. As long as company income exceeds these costs, the company turns a profit. To make sure the company *stays* profitable, payroll and other budgetary expenses are set lower than expected company income. Then, the payroll budget is distributed across employees.

With contributionism, this doesn't change. The overall number for the payroll budget can remain about the same — it's just a case of shuffling the individual pay rates within payroll to conform with appropriate pay ratios. We aren't talking about the confiscation of assets or a heavy tax burden on business, simply an adjustment to how the payroll budget is distributed.

RATIO PAY — HOW IT WORKS

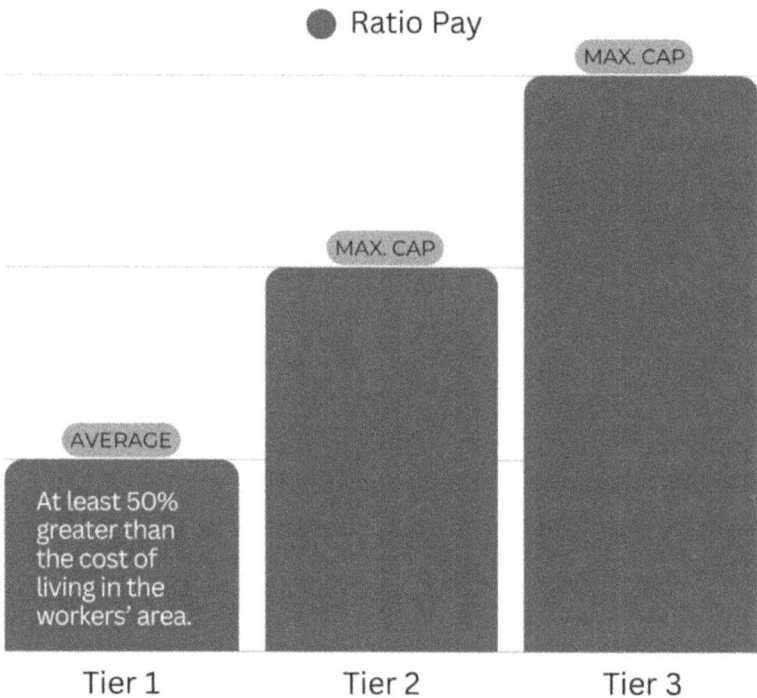

To establish individual pay, the company looks at the expected man-hours of employees in each tier from across the company. Then, the payroll budget is divided up in such a way that correct hourly pay ratios are maintained for employees of each tier. A very simple feat made simpler with computers and AI.

Keep in mind that, because of this hourly approach, positions that are currently salaried would need to have their hours estimated in order to work out pay. Can this be exploited? Yes. I'll address that later on, in the "Loopholes" section.

Ratio pay needn't mean wild fluctuations in pay rates. Currently, businesses set payroll budgets at levels that still allow them to make a profit and that they know they can pay, even if they have a bad year. It's part of the "expense" side of the equation. contributionism doesn't change the payroll budget — it just specifies how to split it up equitably. Just as it is today, pay can be kept at a safe level, ensuring profits are made and that there is "padding" in case of a bad quarter.

Wages

The number of tiers a company has is determined by the size of the company. A small business of a few people can have two tiers, a medium company of 500 employees can have six tiers, and a huge company of over 10,000 employees can have ten. I'll go into this breakdown in more detail shortly in the "Ratio Increases" section.

As I mentioned earlier, "Tier 1" pay is an average of the base pay for employees on the "bottom rung" of the pay ladder. Their pay might not all be exactly the same, and this is fine — "Tier 1" is the average. I'll go into more detail on pay bumps and modifications in the next section. Once this average is determined, it gives us the pay caps for Tier 2 and the tiers above it. Remember: these are maximum caps (with the exception of pay bumps), not minimums. In a medium company, a Tier 3 employee might start off being paid just slightly above the Tier 2 maximum. This leaves room for raises, as well as negotiation between employer and employee.

Profit-Sharing

When profits come in, if there are investors still to be paid out, 50% goes to them, and 50% goes to the company. If there aren't investors to be paid, all of the profits go to the company.

In both cases, of the company's share of the profits:

- Up to 50% may be reinvested back into the company for expansion and development. This money can, of course, be saved away for several years to fund more costly expansions or guard against difficult years.
- The money not reinvested is split up as "bonuses" amongst the company employees and employers, proportionate to their hours and pay tier. If an entry-level employee earns a $5,000 bonus, "Tier 5" employees can make a $25,000 bonus, and a "Tier 10" company owner can make a $50,000 bonus. Larger profits yield larger bonuses for all. Knowing this, workers have a vested interest in making the company profitable.

This payout of profits to employees and investors should come twice a year. With respect to taxes, both the hourly wages and any bonuses are counted toward annual income, as is currently the case.

This sharing of profits doesn't just give employees a stake in the company's success—it also helps to ensure that wages can be set at a level that the company can pay. It allows the company to set "upfront" pay below expected profit margins and then pay the rest out after profits come in. If the company hits a rough patch, perhaps bonus payouts will be impacted, but the upfront pay can remain the same without taking a hit. If the company does extremely well, the employees still see the result of their work in the form of a large bonus on the "backend."

When you're talking about profits, it's important to remember that profits are revenue after expenses. Payroll, shipping, marketing, operating costs — these are all valid expenses.

The issue is, companies will also lump in fines for harmful business practices as expenses, as well as donations to political action committees to influence the election process and bad studies to influence public opinion. These are *not* valid expenses. This is how so many companies get around fines — they simply budget them into their expense budget.

This is what I mentioned before: in our system, anything is legal if you have the money. In the case of corporations, that money is the result of the labor of the company's workers — workers who are not making decisions that pilot the company. These workers should not have their profits reduced because of unethical choices on the part of their bosses.

Therefore, the cost of fines, campaign/lobbying donations, and research that failed peer review but was used anyway should not be considered expenses that decrease the workers' share of profits — instead, they should come from the chunk of profits going back to the business, the profits going to investors, or the wages of the bosses themselves. Plus, the cost of these fines should still be considered "paid" when it comes to investors' ROI (return on investment) cap; this ensures it decreases potential profit rather than simply slowing it down. Pursuing this policy will aid in getting around the "corporate shield doctrine" and force business owners and investors to actually take responsibility for their actions.

Raises and Pay Modifications

Let's take a look at how skilled labor, danger pay, and raises can be accommodated within contributionism. The most important detail to note going in is that pay bumps for skilled labor or danger pay are NOT considered when determining the average Tier 1 pay for the company; they're bonus pay due to the skill/risk involved in doing the job. Employees in higher tiers should not be entitled to extra pay simply because those beneath them are doing work that requires special skills or heightened risk.

For Tier 2 and above, these pay bumps can take them over their base pay cap, allowing specialized skills or extra risk to be rewarded even in higher tiers.

SKILLED LABOR

Jobs qualifying as skilled labor are jobs that cannot be done effectively without specialized training. These are jobs whose description requires at least one of the following:

- A bachelor's degree or higher in a relevant field
- The completion of a recognized apprenticeship or certification in a relevant field
- Having at least three years of experience in a relevant field

These jobs require time and effort to learn, so they require extra compensation in recognition of that investment of time. This skill requirement is partially defined by the company itself — if a company wants to require all their applicants for an entry-level job to have a bachelor's degree plus six years of experience, that's fine; but it does mean that the job will require a skilled labor pay bump.

Workers who are considered skilled labor are paid out at their tier +0.25. So, if a skilled craftsman is employed at entry level (say, a mason, for instance), they would be paid out as if they were at "Tier 1.25". If a master mason is overseeing a group of masons and would usually be paid at Tier 2, they would instead receive "Tier 2.25" pay, and so on.

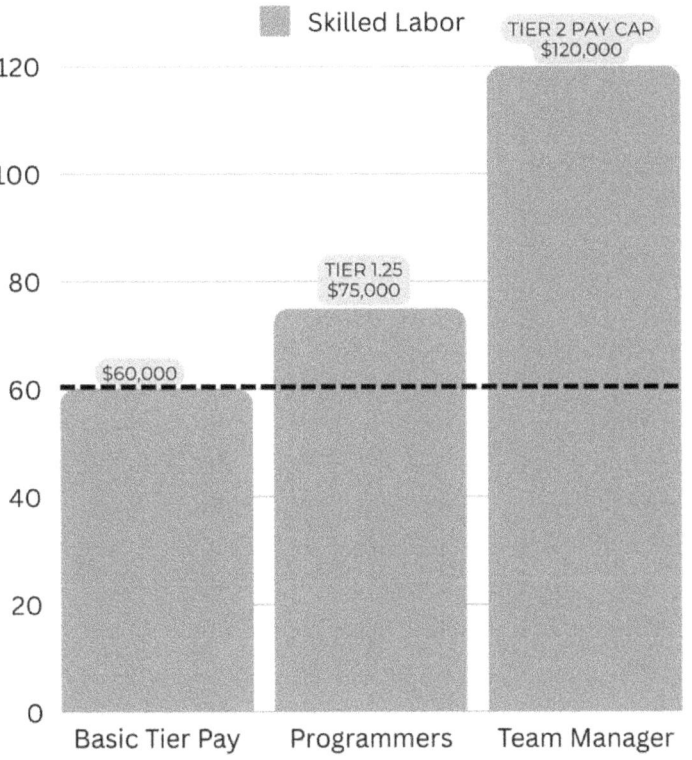

Some companies require special training for all their entry-level employees — a software development company employing programmers, for instance. In this case, their programmers' pay is still considered "Tier 1.25."

Using this example, if an entry-level programmer makes $75k a year, basic Tier 1 pay would be $60k. This is important for calculating the rest of the earnings up the company ladder. If a team manager oversees a group of these programmers, their Tier 2 pay cap is $120k — not $150k. Their pay cap doesn't increase just because the people they supervise have special skills.

In addition to rewarding experience and training, this provides a financial incentive for companies to relax their requirements for entry-level positions. By not requiring a degree and several years of experience for every entry job, they save the money they would have had to spend on a pay bump. This helps to address a frustrating catch-22 (you need experience to get experience) and allows more people a chance to get onto the company ladder.

Danger Pay

Jobs qualifying for danger pay are "jobs whose description entails a significant risk to personal health and safety." This doesn't need to be overly re-thought because many jobs already incorporate danger pay[72]; this would simply stipulate a minimum of how much extra pay they would receive for their contribution. Pay for these jobs works in a similar way as skilled labor: the worker's tier plus 0.25. This can be combined with skilled labor. For instance, a deep-sea welder who has been hired as an entry-level employee would receive double the usual Tier 1 compensation: $1 + 0.25 + 0.25$.

As I've mentioned, for Tier 2 and above, the pay is a maximum. However, this maximum does not include pay bumps for skill or danger! For workers at Tier 2 and above, these pay bumps can take a worker above their "maximum" pay.

---

[72] Logging workers, truck drivers, soldiers in combat zones, firemen, fishers, roofers, farmers, etc.

Raises

Employees in each tier don't all need to be paid the same. Companies should offer incentives for continued work and to reward loyalty — that's just good business. When calculating what "Tier 1 pay" actually is, all entry-level employees' wages (not including skill and danger pay bumps) are averaged. This means that raises for individuals at the bottom "trickle up" by slightly increasing the amount that higher tiers can be paid.

As I touched on earlier, for Tier 2 and up, the pay ratio is a maximum cap. Their raises cannot bring their base pay above this cap. That said, remember that the difference between two adjacent tiers is an entire entry-level worker's wage. Just because someone is at Tier 2 or above doesn't mean their pay must immediately start at their tier's maximum — it might just be a small pay increase from the previous tier, allowing plenty of room for negotiations and raises.

Some Simple Math

Now that we've discussed the basics of how pay works, how do we actually calculate it? Once a business is contributionist, it's fairly simple year to year — they simply have to track the earnings and individual raises of the bottom tier of the company and then adjust wage caps proportionately throughout the business. As it grows, raises can also be given across the business — for example giving the bottom floor a $1/hr. raise, the second tier a $2/hr. raise, and so on up the ladder — increasing the amount those at the top can make.

But how would a business looking to become contributionist determine their pay rates? There are a whole bunch of ways to approach it.

First of all, a company could look at what they're currently paying their entry workers and simply adjust the wages for the tiers above them so that they fit contributionist ratios. This would significantly reduce upfront payroll costs, and the money saved could then be distributed as profit on the backend.

They could alternatively do some "juggling" in order to keep upfront pay high. In this case, they would balance things by lowering wages at the very top and adding them to the bottom until contributionist pay ratios are achieved.

Finally, they could move to contributionism by doing a wage overhaul: starting fresh by calculating wages based on their payroll budget. Does this involve math? Yes. So do most other aspects of business. "It's too complicated to figure out all that pay" is just an excuse to continue not paying people what they're worth. If mega-corporations can coordinate payroll across dozens of departments for tens or hundreds of thousands of employees, this can easily be done.

To demonstrate how figuring out pay within this system is extremely doable, I've whipped up a handy equation for establishing base pay, pay bumps, and tier limits based on the payroll budget:

E = B / ((a + 2b + 3c + 4d + 5e + 6f + 7g + 8h + 9i + 10j) + (0.25P))

Here are what those variables mean:

E = Entry pay

B = Payroll budget

a, b, c, d, e, f, g, h, i, j = Employees at each tier, with "a" being Tier 1 and "j" being Tier 10.

P = Number of pay bumps within the company. Each individual pay bump is counted, so an employee who gets danger pay and skilled labor pay would contribute two pay bumps.

As an example, let's look at a fictional company with 418 employees. A company of this size can have six tiers — meaning we can ignore the variables g, h, i, and j because those tiers aren't available. In this company, workers are distributed like this:

Tier 1 (a) — Entry workers: 370
Tier 2 (b) — Low-level managers and specialty jobs: 30
Tier 3 (c) — General managers: 10
Tier 4 (d) — Department heads/directors: 5
Tier 5 (e) — VPs: 2
Tier 6 (f) — Business owner/president: 1

Within this company, there are 78 workers who are considered skilled labor (one pay bump each), 26 workers performing dangerous jobs (one pay bump each), and nine who are a combination of both (2 pay bumps each). This means that between danger pay and skilled labor pay, there are 122 pay bumps required; 87 for skilled labor and 35 for danger pay.

Let's say that this company has a payroll budget of $30 million each year.

Looking at our formula once more:

```
E = B/((a + 2b + 3c + 4d + 5e + 6f) +
(0.25P))
E = $30 million/((370 + 2(30) + 3(10) + 4(5)
    + 5(2) + 6(1)) + (0.25(122)))
E = $30 million/((370 + 60 + 30 + 20 + 10 +
    6) + (30.5))
E = $30 million/526.5
E = $56,980.05
```

Entry pay for this company can be set at $56,980.05/year (or $28.49/hr if employees work 40-hour weeks for 50 weeks per year). Pay caps for each tier are based on this — so Tier 2 employees can make up to $113,960.10/yr. Tier 3 can make up to $170,940.15/yr. All the way up to the company boss, who can make $341,880.30/yr. The boss can still make an incredible amount of money — $1 million in less than three years — but the people doing the work to make the company run will be brought along with them.

Employees receiving pay bumps will receive an extra 25% of Tier 1 base pay. In this case, that's an extra $14,245.01 each year.

Remember: for the second tier and above, this is the maximum pay. Employees in these tiers don't need to be paid at their maximum, which will allow for even more wiggle room. Also, remember that this is all just salary — before any profits are distributed as bonuses.

Is this perfectly even? No. Can business owners still have huge incomes? Yes. But things are much more ethical and fairer than they are in the system we currently live under.

BUT WHAT ABOUT WAGE FLUCTUATION?

A concern I've heard is that this system could lead to frequent fluctuations in pay. This could happen for two main reasons.

First of all, what happens if you hire new entry-level employees at a lower pay rate than the employees who have been there longer? Won't that reduce average entry pay, meaning reduced pay caps?

This is why these pay caps are maximums, not minimums. It's unfair to bring in new entry-level employees at the same rate as employees who have been working for the company for years. Won't bringing in new workers who are paid less than their more experienced coworkers mean lowering the average pay, thus lowering the pay caps of the higher tiers each time new entry workers are hired? The answer is yes — but not drastically. If employees in these tiers aren't being paid the maximum rate, they will be unaffected even if new entry-level employees are brought in making a little less than their "Tier 1" counterparts who have been with the company longer. If the "Tier 3" maximum is $150k, and a "Tier 3 manager" is being paid $120k, there is $30k worth of wiggle room. That means that the average annual pay for Tier 1 would have to go down by over $10k before any of their income is threatened.

Second, what if there is a year of bad sales with lower profit margins? How could we keep people's pay stable?

This is where profit-sharing comes in. As I mentioned, with our current system, payroll accounts for only a small percentage of gross revenue. If the business takes a hit financially, their profits will be reduced, and their expansion may be slowed — but the wages can remain unimpacted. It already works in our system — we're keeping the payroll the same but altering the way it's distributed. It's okay if payroll is low enough to allow a decent "profit buffer" because the profits are then shared as I described above. Of the business's share of profits, 50% goes to employees as bonuses. This provides stability for wages but still allows employees to have a stake in the business, and they get to share more fairly in the fruits of their labor. As the company grows more profitable, wages for all can be raised at a rate that maintains this buffer.

RATIO INCREASES — FROM SMALL TO LARGE BUSINESSES

So, we've talked a lot about pay for different "tiers" throughout a company. How exactly does this "tier" division work?

A division is made when a person has a group of people working beneath them, whom they oversee *and to whom they provide demonstrably valuable support and direction.*

The limit on the number of tiers is based on the number of workers in the company. As a company grows, more tiers may be added, but these additions must also fulfill the criteria above; they must provide value to the people beneath them. When a company expands, they may choose where they wish to add their new tier. It can be close to the top, near the bottom, or right in the middle. The rest of the positions shift respectively, which means that not just the boss, but also middle and upper management can receive small "bonus raises" if they pilot a small company well and it expands. For instance, if a tier is added in the middle, everyone in the tiers above moves up a tier.

1: A one-person business — no cap on earnings

2: 1–9 employees

3: 10–24 employees

4: 25–99 employees

5: 100–399 employees

6: 400–999 employees

7: 1,000–2,499 employees

8: 2,500–4,999 employees

9: 5,000–9,999 employees

10: 10,000+ employees

You'll note that smaller companies can have fewer tiers. This is because with fewer people working, each worker is doing a larger share of the overall work. In a small business with a boss and four employees, each of those employees is doing a much larger percentage of the work that makes the business run than in a company with five hundred workers. Additionally, as a business gets larger, so do the responsibilities the boss faces. This increased responsibility entitles them to increased compensation.

I've outlined the tier structure and employee requirements below. Once again, each "tier" number represents the amount that the company head may make compared to their base-level workers. Tier 4 means they may make four times the amount. Tier 6 means six times, etc.

As the company grows, more tiers are added to reflect management positions, department heads, etc. And remember: this is just the basic pay structure. From here, pay can (and should) be modified to account for raises or differences between individual jobs of that tier, as described above.

AN EXAMPLE

Let's put all of this into more concrete terms by looking at a very small business. We'll imagine a bookstore as an example.

TIER 1 — SIMPLE SELF-EMPLOYMENT

Solo Operation

The store opens, and it's run by one person. This person, as a one-person show, gets to keep all of their own profits. Alternatively, if a group decides to run the shop as an equal partnership, they can all make roughly the same amount per hour.

TIER 2 – HIRING WORKERS

1–9 Employees

Eventually, the store becomes more popular and busier and requires several employees to be hired, whom the owner directly oversees. The owner supports their employees by helping with duties, ordering stock, working on accounting, taking care of inventory, etc. while the employees focus on the process of selling and stocking books. The owner is able to make twice what their employees do.

Included in these employees are floor workers and individuals who handle payroll and marketing.

In some situations, a Tier 2 company may need shift managers. If this is the case, they're still considered Tier 1 employees,but remember: pay rates can be negotiated! These managers may start making a bit more than the employees they manage, and their pay is considered when finding the average "Tier 1 pay."

TIER 3 – HIRING SHIFT MANAGERS, PAYROLL, AND HR

10–24 Employees

Hiring managers

This is the level where business owners begin hiring managers.

Tier 1: Entry-level workers. Tier 2: Managers for shifts, payroll, HR, or marketing. Tier 3: Business owner/manager.

TIER 4 – EXPANSION

25–99 Employees. Expansion to greater size or greater area

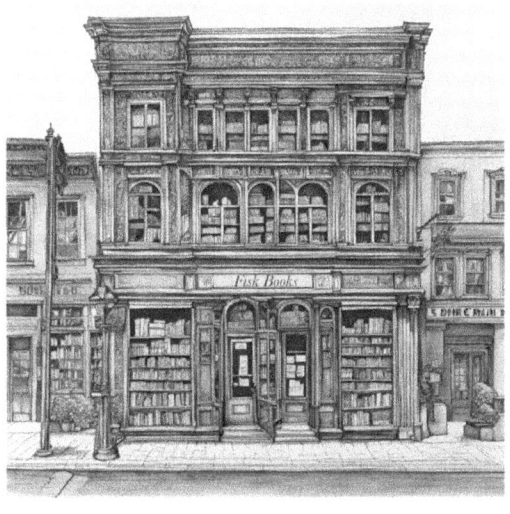

Tier 4 is reached when the company branches out to multiple locations and must hire general managers to oversee those locations. Or, in the case of something like a growing factory, it's reached when the operation expands enough that they need managers who oversee different areas of production, like shipping vs. manufacturing vs. an HR team manager.

Tier 3 managers here are "managers of managers," and they have the responsibility for their location's success.

Tier 1: Entry workers. Tier 2: Floor managers and team managers. Tier 3: General manager. Tier 4: Company owner.

TIER 5 — DIVISION HEADS

100–399 Employees

This tier consists of hiring specialist heads to lead each department of a company expanding into more areas.

In this tier, "division heads" is a relatively loose term. Each company is different and has different management needs — this extra tier provides some flexibility to fit the company's requirements.

Tier 1: Entry workers. Tier 2: Floor managers and team managers. Tier 3: General Manager. Tier 4: Division Heads. Tier 5: Company owner.

TIER 6 — REGIONAL EXECUTIVES

400–999 Employees

As the company expands, they hire executives to oversee groups of stores or business locations or to oversee marketing and business in a specific area.

Tier 1: Workers. Tier 2: Floor managers and team managers. Tier 3: General Manager. Tier 4: Division Heads. Tier 5: Regional Executives. Tier 6: Company owner.

TIER 7 — NATIONAL EXECUTIVES

1,000–2,499 Employees

Once the company goes international, executives are hired to oversee entire groups of regions.

Tier 1: Workers. Tier 2: Floor managers and team managers. Tier 3: General Manager. Tier 4: Division Heads. Tier 5: Regional Executives. Tier 6: National Executives. Tier 7: Company owner.

TIERS 8 -10 — RESPONSIBILITY

Employees — Tier 8: 2,500–4,990; Tier 9: 5,000–9,999; Tier 10: 10,000+

Tiers 8–10 increase based on expansion. As the company grows, the company may need more than seven tiers. It would be absurd to assume that one outline can foresee all needs and eventualities. After

Tier 7, once a company hits the required number of employees, they may add another tier, so long as they can justify it as a position that is demonstrably aiding the workers beneath them.

> This "increased pay ratio for increased workers" is both fair and sensible. These are not small jumps in employees, and with more and more workers depending upon the boss's leadership, the boss's responsibility increases. If the CEO is facilitating a high-quality standard of living for ten thousand employees or more in return for their contribution, it is fair to provide that CEO with a little extra compensation.

BENEFITS AND HEALTHCARE

Right now, there are millions of Americans who don't have access to affordable healthcare. As of 2024, the number was 27 million.[73] 73% of them have at least one full-time worker in their family.[55] Many of these people work for companies whose upper-level employees have excellent healthcare.[74] Is this an argument against excellent healthcare? No. Of course not. But when two people are working similar hours, this huge difference in quality is ethically unacceptable. Especially when the one without healthcare is also paid far less and, therefore, has less to spend on things that would promote health and longevity.

---

73 The Department of Health and Human Services and The Kaiser Family Foundation both released statistics on this. See bibliography for data.

74 While many workers are lucky to get poor healthcare plans from reluctant insurance providers, executive health screenings are incredibly proactive and comprehensive. The Mayo Clinic's executive health screening is conducted by a dedicated physician, it can last a few days and provides options for cosmetic surgery and time at their "rejuvenate spa." See bibliography for details.

Beyond that, as the cost of healthcare becomes more and more extortionary, we're seeing an emergence of a new healthcare-based form of feudalism. People are being forced to stay in jobs because leaving means losing their health insurance. Some may argue that they should simply find another job with healthcare, but many places of employment that do offer it only do so after the first year. This means rolling the dice on a year without coverage. Depending on the individual's situation, that may not be feasible. They are forced to remain working and bound in service to their modern "lord" — the company.

TWO OPTIONS: BASIC ALLOWANCE OR UNIVERSAL HEALTHCARE

The ideal situation is to take some of the extra wealth that's being spread around and taxed and use it to provide healthcare for our citizens. This can be done within our current system by providing citizens with a basic healthcare "allowance" that they could spend at any healthcare provider. This approach of providing an allowance (rather than setting up government-run medical institutions) would serve to foster competition between providers to promote high-quality healthcare. They'd still be independent entities, and citizens could choose where to spend their healthcare allowance. The healthcare system remains a free market — just one that more people have access to. It also means that individuals with the funds could spend more to augment their care.

This isn't a new idea — similar systems have already been successfully implemented in other developed countries including Germany and Australia.[75] It's worth mentioning that compared to other high-income nations, the U.S. ranks last on key measures of

---

[75] Germany's and Australia's departments of health both have better health outcomes and lower costs than our own. See bibliography for reports.

effectiveness, while at the same time somehow costing the most.[76] Once again, would it not make a country "great" to have a long life expectancy and to be able to say, "We don't simply let our citizens die because they're poor"?

The less "noble" but more productivity-based alternative is: if someone gets healthcare, everyone gets healthcare. It's as straightforward as it sounds — a very "treat others how you'd like to be treated" policy. In this version, health insurance is still tied to business, but if the company provides it for the boss, they provide similar insurance for the workers. The boss can, of course, use some of their own money (which their workers helped them to make) to augment their plan should they so desire.

Additionally, in order to undo healthcare feudalism, health insurance should begin after a month of work for the company, rather than a year. This version may be a little more complicated and require more oversight, and it may not add to "what it means to be a citizen," but it does tie healthcare to employment to discourage idle people from draining the system. Exceptions could, of course, be made for the disabled or for those with a legitimate reason for being unable to work — something we already do today.

I personally prefer a universal healthcare allowance, but I know that there are plenty of folks out there who are concerned with people mooching off the system. This option would keep health insurance tied to work but give people more flexibility to leave jobs they hate, knowing

---

76 The Commonwealth Fund report entitled "US ranks last on key health care measures compared with other high-income nations, despite spending the most" really says it all. See bibliography for article.

that they can find insurance elsewhere and that they don't have to wait a year for it to kick in.

TRANSPARENCY

It's likely so obvious that it goes without saying, but I'll say it anyway, just in case: contributionism requires pay transparency to function. This accountability is a fair ask — after all, the workers making the products should be entitled to know how much money those products are generating as well as seeing how much they're being paid for their time compared to the boss. Without transparency, how can an honest, hardworking American tell if they're being swindled?

In contributionism, current pay rates and profits should be updated every quarter and made easily available to employees on the company site or payroll software. For companies that are small enough to have neither, general breakdowns should be posted in break rooms along with more detailed info available upon request. Secrecy and obscurity serve only as cover for the people at the top of the business to reap unfair rewards from their workers' labor.

FAQs

Congrats on making it this far! You've read through everything you need to for a real "nuts and bolts" understanding of the theory behind contributionism, as well as how it works. Now, let's proactively take a look at a whole bunch of questions that can (and should!) arise. If you had questions while reading this book, hopefully, they will be answered here.

SO... ARE INVESTMENTS JUST LOANS NOW?

No. Sure, investment no longer entitles you to permanent profit from the company's work simply because you bought shares once. But it does entitle you to a much larger profit than most loans do. To break it down:

Loans: As of November of 2024, the average interest rate for a business loan from a bank was a little under 10%.[77] Online loans can get a little bit higher, so let's just be generous to the lender in this scenario and call it 15%. A borrower is on the hook to pay this back, but if paid back within a reasonable time frame, the lender doesn't stand to earn a fortune. Even if the borrower took five years to pay it back, the lender would only make a 75% return. On the other hand, the borrower is "on the hook" for this money. They owe it to the lender and must pay it back, whether the venture succeeds or fails.

Contributionist Investments: Just like now, the business is responsible for reporting to the investor to ensure that they're doing

---

[77] This rate can vary based on the type of loan and the recipient's credit. See bibliography for average business loan rates as of 2024.

their due diligence while running the company. If the venture fails, the borrower does not remain in debt. The investment is simply a loss. For this additional risk, there is an additional reward: under contributionism, a low-risk investment can provide a 100% return. A high-risk investment provides a 300% return. Compared to the returns that loans receive, this is very fair compensation for the risk.

How is the Riskiness of an Investment Calculated?

Investment risk assessment is an area of opportunity for those who seek to bar certain businesses from success or for corruption to breed. Therefore, the risk must be formally defined based on field, founder experience, market saturation, etc. These are the same markers used today by investors to gauge whether to invest in a venture — this sort of risk assessment is something we've proven ourselves capable of doing.[78] We simply need to apply it to investment in a contributionist model.

What About Existing Stocks? What About Retirements and Personal Investments?

Stocks that are currently in circulation will be treated as though the investment just happened. The price of the shares will be assessed, and the companies these stocks represent will pay the shareholders profits as previously described until they are fully paid out. For the ROI caps on these stocks, companies can be assessed based on the current risk of buying stock in them. Once these returns have been hit, shareholders will

---

[78] There are many forms of risk assessment currently used, including value at risk (VaR), dynamic risk assessment, and standard deviation. There are even automated risk assessment tools available. See bibliography for more details.

be "bought out," as previously described, and the shares will go back to the company, spurring growth and wages.

Keep in mind, money management companies can still exist, using large funds from many citizens as investment capital. They simply need to follow the contributionist model and continue finding businesses to support once their shares have been bought out.

BUT I FEEL I DESERVE TO HAVE MORE THAN EVERYONE ELSE!

No, that's not a question, BUT, if you *must* be high maintenance, that's still possible. If you amass wealth, you can still invest it. You'll simply need to continue providing support to new businesses as your shares are eventually bought out. Even a low-risk investment can double your money — not bad for no direct work and minimal oversight. One can still amass great wealth under contributionism; they just need to continue providing their support to businesses.

I would also encourage you to examine your philosophy. There was a famous study done in 2010 called the Deaton-Kahneman study.[79a] They asked participants across the socio-economic spectrum to rate how happy they were with their lives, finding a steady increase in happiness and satisfaction as income increased — up to $70k (give or take a little depending on location). Adjusted for inflation, that's about $108k in 2024. After $108k, happiness and satisfaction tend to level off and stay about the same, regardless of income. There is a study that challenges this,[78b] coming to a different answer by using different methods, but the authors agree that *unhappiness,* despair, and misery disappear after $108k. Regardless of where you land on these two studies — consider

---

79 See bibliography for details on these studies. The "conflicting study" I mentioned as 79b is highly questionable — feel free to find out more via the bibliography.

just how many cultures have their own parables and cautionary stories about miserable misers.

To say all this in a more straightforward way: if you're still unhappy after exceeding $108k a year, making more money probably won't fix your problem. If you're still feeling unfulfilled or unhappy, it's likely because the things you're focusing on and prioritizing aren't giving you everything you need. Very often, prioritizing money over other, deeper pursuits like community engagement, time with friends and family, or creative endeavors is the very thing that causes this unhappiness.

WHAT ABOUT PAY FOR PUBLIC SERVICES AND GOVERNMENT POSITIONS?

First of all, contributionism starts with business. Applying it to business through the free market by voting with our wallets is enough to make a huge impact. That is the first step because it's the more actionable one. But keep in mind, a huge number of jobs are in the public sector, including public services and government. It makes sense to also base these jobs on contributionist values. In the case of government officials at the top, it ensures they have a monetary incentive to serve the people as a whole. In the case of public services, it ensures that the jobs pay well enough to attract top talent.

In order to accomplish this within public services and government, a different approach must be used than for business. This is because these jobs cover a huge range of positions — school cafeteria workers, sanitation supervisors, firefighters, civil engineering, public works directors, senators, etc. — far more than are included in a corporation. On top of that, these positions are present across the country, with different living expenses in different places. Because of this, we need a more flexible pay scale. Rather than having rigid, defined tiers, I propose using a "government minimum" and "government maximum" pay system.

Similar to private jobs, public services and government pay should be tied to the average income of the country's citizens. However, instead of being tied to the average of the lowest-earning citizens (like in business), a government "minimum pay" should be established based on the average income of the bottom 90% of earners. This range applies to all tax-funded positions in both government and public service.

Historically, the wealthy have time and time again been able to gain disproportionate control over politics through bribery and campaign finance dealings. By basing government income off the bottom 90%, we ensure that politicians have a vested interest in ensuring that employees are paid fairly across the board so that all the wealth doesn't consolidate at the top. It provides them with an incentive to look out for the vast majority — because by doing so, they can increase what they can be paid themselves.

Furthermore, this approach would mean that even low-level public service jobs are well-paid. The average pay of the entire bottom 90% is by definition higher than an average entry-level job, encouraging hardworking people to apply, attracting talented workers, motivating them to do good work, and increasing the quality of services that the public receives.

On the other end of the spectrum is "maximum pay," which is three times the minimum. This may be a lower cap than private business — with large corporations topping out at "Tier 10" — but remember: with business, the maximum cap is based on the average of their *lowest-level* employees. With government jobs, maximum pay is based on the average income of the bottom *90%* of Americans. This means that government minimum pay will be a bit higher than "Tier 1" at a business.

Within this minimum–maximum range, there is flexibility in terms of which positions get what pay. So long as they fall within these parameters, departments have the ability to decide pay for each position, with entry-level workers getting close to the minimum and department leaders, senators, and the president receiving closer to the maximum. It also means that there is flexibility to take other important things into account, like the difference in the cost of living from region to region.

Because of the way in which the "government minimum" is calculated, even the lowest-paid government workers can remain comfortably middle class. As of 2024, the average annual income was around $56k — better than what most entry-level government jobs are currently paying. Sanitation services, postal workers, DMV clerks[80] — suddenly, folks actually have a financial incentive to take these jobs. They can build a life and see that their work is actually allowing them to do the things they want.

We get what we pay for, and by allowing the rich to both dodge taxes *and* not pay their employees well, you wind up with poorly funded government services. The answer is not to cut these services to reduce taxes even more because it isn't the tax rate that's the root issue. I'll go into this shortly in the "How do we pay for this?" section coming up.

Emergency services and teachers will also be paid well, with firefighters and the police getting a danger pay bump as described above, and teachers receiving a skilled labor pay bump. For government positions, these pay bumps are 50% of minimum pay, similar to how they

---

80 On average, each of these jobs makes: sanitation — $33k (2024); postal worker — $41k (2023); DMV clerk — $36.5k (2024). See bibliography for more details.

work within private business. With this being the case, all of these jobs will guarantee you a solid middle- or upper-middle-class life.

Pay bumps for skilled work and danger pay would also apply to public service jobs. Assuming that in education teachers are paid just the bare minimum, after their pay bump they would be paid 50% more than the average earnings of the bottom 90% (minimum + 50% of minimum for skilled labor). Using the $56k figure from above, this would put teachers' pay at around $84k each year. Compare that to the average public-school teacher's pay in 2025, which is about $59k.[81] Being a teacher would be a job that's rewarding both mentally AND financially, attracting and retaining good teachers and thus raising the standard of education.

When first implementing this policy, the pay rate is calculated based on the bottom 90%'s average income from the previous four years. This rate is used for four more years, at which point it's recalculated based on the average incomes from those years. For instance, if this policy was implemented in 2029, the average income of the bottom 90% from 2025 to 2029 would be used. This rate would be used for four years until 2033.

In 2033, the rate would be adjusted to reflect the average income from 2029 to 2033. This prevents fluctuations in pay from year to year and ensures that one bad year doesn't tank government wages. This may seem like a lot of math, but it really isn't. We have machines capable of calculating all of this in less than an hour — even our smartphones have greater calculating power than the computers that landed people on the moon and got them back again. There is no reason that these numbers couldn't be found.

---

81 According to data from Salary.com. See bibliography for more details.

WHO WILL BE MONITORING CORRUPTION UNDER CONTRIBUTIONISM?

One additional change that I would pitch within the government: due to repeated cycles of corruption, we know that bribery and other forms of unethical compensation are common in the halls of power. We have checks and balances within the government, but little in the way of checking the government against corruption — especially with the way our news no longer presents an objective viewpoint. What we need is an organization that specifically oversees elected officials to ensure that illicit funds aren't being taken.

This group's main representatives are voted on by the people, and they function as a sort of IRS for government officials and government spending. They make their information available to the public and prosecute government officials caught up in bribery. Their funding comes from a percentage of overall taxes, which cannot be changed by the rest of the government once it's set. Decisions about raising or lowering this funding are voted upon by the people — in exactly the same way that we directly vote upon certain laws in each election cycle.

Yes, this requires the formation of an organization — but the money saved in both the short term (through clamping down on corruption) and the long term (by ensuring politicians continue to serve the people), more than makes up for the cost. This is not an organization that oversees the government and influences their decision-making — giving a non-elected group that power would be problematic. Instead, it simply acts as an IRS to audit government officials' income to guard against illegal compensation and make their financing public knowledge.

WHO KEEPS TRACK OF EVERYTHING?

One of the great perks of the U.S. is our parks. If you go to any national park — and many state parks — in the country, you'll see CCC projects. The Civilian Conservation Corps was founded as part of the New Deal to provide jobs. These civilian workers created some impressive and enduring infrastructure that has a positive impact to this day. The same type of thing can be done with keeping business honest and ethical.

Now, I'm no advocate for bureaucracy. It tends to be slow and lumbering. But like laws, it's a necessary evil when people don't act ethically on their own. These organizations would not all need to be built from scratch but could easily be rolled into the purview of existing oversight organizations within the government, such as the FTC. As a bonus, any extra personnel required would provide work for the many people who stand to lose their jobs to AI.

CONTRIBUTIONISM PROPOSES THREE BODIES:

INVESTMENT APPRAISERS

Investment appraisers are the ones who are approached by businesses raising funds. They approve or deny (deny in the case of scams) the request, provide a reason, and assign a risk value. This risk value assures investors and allows them to know what their return may be. This can easily be accomplished as part of business oversight organizations that already exist.

This is inherently an area that can be twisted to bar certain groups from being eligible for investment funds. This sort of discrimination can be brought to the courts, similarly to loan discrimination.

These appraisers can simply be an addition to the Department of Business and Trade or the FTC and paid like other government positions.

GOVERNMENT OVERSIGHT

This is the group I mentioned in the government pay section. It focuses on campaign finance and public servant revenue streams. It makes complete sense to insist that our elected officials are transparent and accountable to the people, and this group provides that oversight.

This group would likely need to be organized as its own entity. It is outside the current government hierarchy to prevent conflicting interests, though it is of course bound by our laws and must answer for its actions. The leadership is elected on a state-by-state basis.

This group is paid the same way as other government employees, with one large exception: half of anything they find and prove to be bribery or illicit funds is distributed to the department as bonuses, exactly like profits are for business. The other half goes into the tax pool. As with the business oversight group, this provides a strong monetary incentive to crack down on corruption. It also means that this department may be paid slightly more than standard government jobs, ensuring that it attracts great workers. Finally, it makes attempting to bribe members of this department very difficult and risky — they simply have to report the bribe and it's theirs.

This organization does NOT have the authority to tell governing officials how to govern. They specifically act as an IRS for government officials, ensuring they are transparent with their funds and campaign financing.

BUSINESS OVERSIGHT

This group oversees hours claimed by businesses and also approves the addition of new tiers to the company. They ensure that tiers being added are actually contributing to their subordinates, as well as ensuring that bosses aren't fudging their numbers, underpaying workers, or otherwise attempting to cheat their employees.

This group can form as an organization within our existing structure as part of the Department of Labor and work on a state-by-state basis. It's paid the same way as any other government position.

The head of this organization for each state is elected by the people of that state.

This department receives 10% of any money they recover from businesses or executives trying to defraud employees. This provides a monetary incentive to look out for those at most risk of being cheated out of the fruits of their labor.

Corruption will try to happen. Looking at history, we know it's human to desire both an easier life and greater compensation. It's a fact that we must plan for, and these groups work to slow corruption's advance.

HOW DO WE PAY FOR ALL THIS?

Remember what we discussed earlier? How the top 10% hold about 70% of our nation's wealth, and the bottom half splits 2.5%... People at the top and the bottom both treat "taxes" like a bad word — but taxes are *how* a society works together to accomplish things. It's a pooling of resources so that we can accomplish more than we could on our own. The thing is, when wealth is distributed the way it is now, we *need* to tax the wealthy more; they're the ones with all the money! What are you going to do — make the half of society splitting 2.5% of our wealth pay for everything? They can't afford it! In a society where there is such a huge gap in wealth, the rich hate taxes because taxes take a huge percentage of their income while the poor hate taxes because even the smaller percentage they're paying stretches them very thin.

To make matters worse, the services our taxes provide seem to be deteriorating. Because of our country's history of tax breaks for the rich and the consolidation of money at the top, we have had to make repeated cuts to government programs to continue to afford them. This drop in funding has — predictably — led to a drop in quality, adding insult to injury.

As I've mentioned, unequal tax rates are a necessity when you live in a nation where CEOs make 344 times what their workers do. They're a backend fix. By instead fixing the real problem — wild income inequality — tax rates can be made much more equitable.

As a quick example, imagine a person who makes $50k each year. If they are taxed at 20%, they spend $10k on taxes — leaving $40k. Let's say that $35k is enough to cover all their living expenses. When all is said and done, that leaves almost nothing for entertainment, fun experiences, self-advancement, or savings. If they manage to be extremely frugal and save the entire leftover $5k each year — never going out to eat, never going on vacation, never spending money for entertainment, never taking time off work, never buying a plane ticket to see family — they could pay off a house in 80 years.

But… what would it look like if this person was paid $75k each year? At a 20% tax rate, they would spend $15k on taxes — leaving $60k to cover their living expenses. With their $35k living expenses, this leaves them a full $25k. They could spend $5k on experiences, put $5k into retirement, *and* pay off a house in less than 27 years. On top of that, the government is receiving an extra $5k to fund important civil services.

If taxes stress you out, just remember: it isn't the tax rate that's making you angry, it's the fact that your pay is so low that taxes have become a significant burden.

This is how we pay for our services: by insisting that workers be paid fairly for the contribution of their time and effort. The bottom 50% of the workforce is made up of about 80 million people. If we applied my example above to all of them, that's an extra 400 *billion* dollars every year, with more money left over for each of them. This is simplified math, but it does serve to illustrate my point: when wages rise, taxation burdens people less while generating a greater amount of money for higher-quality government services. When wealth evens out, we no longer *need* to tax the rich at such high rates — because other people *actually have money to tax.* The only reason we're having so many issues with taxes and poorly funded public services is because, through decades of careful lobbying and campaign finance, the rich have succeeded in placing more and more of the financial responsibility for this country upon the shoulders of everyone else. Through its policy of fair pay, contributionism decreases the burden of taxes, while at the same time raising the standards for public services.

As with every period of change, there may be difficulties or shortcomings. I've already mentioned the need for oversight of income and pay, as well as our responsibility to look after the older population in the event of adverse impacts from changes to the investment system. If the rising wealth of our citizens is not able to finance all the changes needed, a small portion of the defense budget can easily make up the difference.

WHAT ABOUT THE DEFENSE BUDGET?

First of all, just to really get an idea of what we're talking about here — in 2023, our defense budget was $816 billion.[82] If you add up the annual defense spending of the next *ten* countries, it comes to about $802 billion.[83] If we cut our defense budget in *half*, we'd still be spending over *75% more* on defense than China, the runner-up.

Do we need to maintain a military to ensure our security? Absolutely. It's foolish to assume that we'll never face threats. But the defense budget might be able to have the fat trimmed if it's necessary to improve the home front. Not just due to its excess, but also due to the quickly evolving nature of warfare. Spending billions on an expensive army that runs on oil — a quickly dwindling resource — is a study in resource mismanagement. Military spending (after taking care of our citizens' retirement) should be focused on research & development, veterans' support, and global defense.

I know that this will ruffle a few war-hawk feathers but allow me to pose a few questions. First, whom are we defending? The answer should be, "our citizens." Second, what are we defending them from? In the case

---

82 The U.S. Defense budget for 2024 is linked in the bibliography for more data on military expenditure.

83 See bibliography for information on how the U.S. defense budget stacks up against other advanced nations.

of terrorism or other attacks, the answer is death. In the case of using our military to secure resources, the answer is hardship and scarcity.

By allocating money to ensure support for retirement, we are quite literally defending the aging population from hardship and death by providing money for healthcare, housing, food, and other necessities. This is one of the most noble uses of our defense budget imaginable because it allows us to preserve the lives of our citizens without inflicting death and suffering upon others.

By allocating money to an elected group whose job is to oversee government finance and crack down on bribery, we defend ourselves from an insidious force that traditional defense spending has never been able to fight corruption. People tend to focus on the easy-to-see threats; threats that come from the outside. But one of the main factors in the fall of Rome was corruption eating it away from within.[84] Regardless of the defense budget, if our country falls to division and infighting, we won't have a country any longer.

The U.S. military is so powerful and so highly funded that even shaving a couple hundred billion off the budget would leave our defense budget twice as high as that of China. At the same time, it would provide funds to solidify our nation so we can spring forward into the future from a stronger position. It's worth mentioning here that the evolving nature of warfare means that the country with the best technology often wins — by using contributionism to invest in our nation's future, we set ourselves up to produce citizens who have the education and the means to help us maintain our technological edge.

---

84 Rome's political corruption mirrors our own in many ways. See bibliography for articles on how Rome's corrupt government led to its downfall, as well as how Romans tried to fight against it.

LOOPHOLES

Since the existence of the wealthy, one of their favorite pastimes has been figuring out sneaky ways to play the system. Knowing this, a few loopholes are proactively addressed below. Keep in mind, now we're getting to "responses to trickery." There may be a little light math. If you're averse to that — well, I'd recommend getting better. Corporations, banks, and politicians all use math to screw you over. The better you understand relevant math, the more prepared you are to protect yourself from injustice and predatory behavior.

FUDGING TIME

As we discussed before, to make hourly wages compatible with salaries, we have to estimate the hours of full-time salaried positions. This can be accomplished by assuming salaried employees work full-time — 40 hours a week, as of writing this. Any time worked over this by a salaried employee can be reported each week. But what's to prevent upper-level employees from simply reporting extra hours every week? We know from human history that there is a common desire for self-enrichment with minimal work. This is one of the first glaring loopholes. The answer has two parts: records and a cap.

First off, reporting extra hours consists of officially recording what you did and how long it took. It's submitted in the same way that an expense is. If this is done consistently and the person is claiming considerably more hours than expected, it could be a red flag for the business oversight group, who may choose to audit the claims for false reporting.

The second part is an hour cap. For hourly employees, our current overtime and weekly hour limit laws still apply as usual. For salaried positions, there's also a cap at reporting 60 hours per week. Why is this fair? As an example, if you run a small business with 50 employees, you can make four times the hourly entry pay. Being the boss may take lots of work — perhaps you do put in the full 60 hours each week.

At that point, you could be making six times what one of your 40-hours-a-week entry-level employees makes each week. If you require an extra five hours a week on top of this, that time is unpaid. This encourages efficiency in management and discourages time theft against the workers who make the company function. In an ideal world, it would also encourage business owners to take a breather each week. To pause and appreciate the life going on around them so that they don't miss out on the things they're working for because they're too busy at work. I can't force people to do things that make them happy though, so who knows if that'll happen.

PART-TIMERS

Why not fill the company with tons of people, each working five hours a week? That gets your employee numbers up, potentially putting you into a higher tier as a company, while paying for the same number of hours. This would hurt the workers by incentivizing the greedy to provide terrible hours. Contributionism addresses this by stating that a worker must be working at least 30 hours a week and getting full-time employment benefits to count toward the overall employee number. To avoid making it harder to find a part-time job, two part-time workers whose weekly hours add up to 30 or more may be counted together for the purposes of the overall employee number — each position is considered a "half employee."

RUSHING

What's to stop a company that is close to the next tier from hiring a few more entry-level employees just so that everyone above can move up a pay tier? So long as it doesn't decrease the earnings of the "bottom floor," this is alright. Any wages going to hire folks in the added tier must come from company profits, or from the pay rate of the top tier. This is a critical point because it prevents bosses from simply dropping entry wages in order to add employees so that they can increase the pay cap at the top. This means that to some extent, company profitability must justify additional tiers, not just employee count and function.

MINI COMPANIES

Okay, so someone wants to game the system by making a bunch of little companies. If they have one huge company, in which they employ

---

To break it down:

For the sake of simplicity, let's say that working 60 hours a week, the boss is able to make a meaningful contribution to each of their twelve companies.

That's five hours a week at each company. If their Tier 1 employees each make $50k a year, working 40-hour weeks, the boss could make $37,500 a year from each company by working five-hour weeks.

Across twelve companies, that's $450k, working 60-hour weeks.

Had the boss gone the straightforward route, they could work for 40 hours a week and make $500k per year.

11,000 people, they can earn ten times the salary of their entry-level employees. If they make twelve mini companies, each with 500 people, they can make six times as much as their entry-level employees (500 employees is tier 6). If they pay the same entry wages, they could make 70 times as much as an entry-level employee, right? 12 x 6 = 70. This doesn't end up working out — as described above, the pay is based on hours worked and is only counted if the person is making a meaningful contribution to their subordinates.

FREELANCERS

Why not just hire freelancers and pay them less than Tier 1 employees? Because the freelancers are independent contractors rather than official employees, their rate would be between them and the business. This could increase production without costing as much, without decreasing the Tier 1 average pay, and without having to offer the same benefits. All raises could be directed to official employees in order to increase the executives' potential earnings, and the freelancers would be left to take what they're given or go elsewhere.

In this way, a company of ten could contract 100 freelancers, soak up most of the profits of their labor, and pay them terribly. This raises some obvious concerns because it could lead to an employment structure where vast numbers of workers are essentially temping at their jobs, working as "self-employed" and contracting out to the company for reduced pay and no benefits. I hear my free-market readers saying, "But they can just quit."

Well, a vast number of necessary jobs, though important, do not require much experience or training to fill. If enough companies pursued this policy, many people in difficult financial situations would be left with little choice — they would be forced into a position where they can choose to take one of these bad jobs or not have any job at all. We know from history that desperation is often abused in the name of profits.[85] That's not what contributionism is about.

In order to prevent this, contributionism looks at the type of work being performed:

- If it's directly related to the services or goods the company sells — like drivers for Uber or freelance video editors for film production companies — the freelancer is considered a company employee. They are, after all, doing the work that makes the company run. If they're entry-level, their wages are factored into the Tier 1 average. Entry-level or not, they are also entitled to their share of the company's profits and healthcare.
- If it's unrelated, such as a tech company hiring cleaners or caterers for events, or an interior designer for a new office space, these folks may be hired and paid as is currently done, negotiating pay rates on their own. This is an area that could lead to underpaying, but it's no worse than the current system. Keep in mind that if services are being provided by an outside company, then that company has its own pay scale.

UNDERPAYING THE MIDDLE

Since these ratios are caps, not minimums, it would be theoretically possible for a boss at a Tier 10 company to pay all their middle management just over entry pay, then disburse that saved money to the entry-level employees and then themself. This is unlikely, as middle management would have little incentive to stay. This is where the free

---

85 I really feel like this one is so obvious that I don't need to link specific examples, but check out the bibliography for more.

market does come to the rescue — if pay gets bad enough, it's much harder to stop a middle-management strike. Ratio pay caps may not provide the middle with a "minimum wage," but neither do any laws that exist now. What these caps will provide is transparency in the maximum rates, which can serve as a benchmark for negotiations.

JUMPING SHIP

What's to prevent businesses from simply moving overseas? That would allow them to use cheap labor and keep a mountain of profit. The issue this creates is a hemorrhaging of jobs, making employment harder to come by. We're already fighting this in our current system. To combat all this, any company outsourcing their labor in order to get around fairly paying their workers should pay an additional "flight tax" to sell their goods in the country. This is essentially a selective tariff that is aimed specifically at companies who are attempting to get around contributionist practices by moving their manufacturing overseas.

This money should then be used by the government to offset any unemployment difficulties that arise while new businesses take the place of the ones that left. These new businesses will have the advantage of being able to sell their goods at a lower price since they're not dealing with this tax — offering domestic companies an edge over the ones who left.

Beyond that, they'll be benefiting from eventually owning all their profits, further bringing costs down and lending them another edge. Once these businesses are established and jobs have returned, the additional "flight tax" money from the transition can go back into public services and infrastructure.

AUTOMATION

Replacing jobs with automation will soon be the fastest way to make more money. It allows you to both be more productive and hire fewer entry-level employees. Fewer employees means you can pay each one more, leading to overall higher pay for yourself. Yes, this means the remaining entry-level employees will be paid quite well — as contributionism intends. But it also means that huge numbers of entry-level employees will experience a 100% pay decrease as they get laid off.

This is a problem that is not unique to contributionism. It looms on the horizon for any economic system because we're in uncharted territory technologically. The industrial revolution included, never before have we stood to lose so many jobs due to technology. Contributionism deals with this better than capitalism by ensuring that at least the remaining workers are paid well, but our relationship to labor is changing quickly, and our systems need to change to keep up. The proposal I offer is simple: each job that is replaced by automation is still treated as a job. Its "pay rate" is set at half of "Tier 1" pay (though automated jobs are not considered when finding average "Tier 1" pay). This half-pay rate is required to be paid in an "automation tax." The company keeps the other half.

When it comes time to distribute profits as bonuses, the automated job gets half of a "Tier 1" share of the bonus. Until the machine automating the job is paid for, all of this share of the profits can go toward that. Once the machine is paid off, that half once again goes toward this automation tax.

The money generated by this tax is then used to aid the unemployed or perhaps eventually fund a universal basic income as the number of jobs continues to decline. By only requiring half the wage of the job it replaced, business owners still stand to increase profits and pay by automating, while also mitigating the negative effects of widespread unemployment caused by mass automation. Keep in mind, technology is advancing rapidly — in ten years, we may need to reassess this tax rate. As more jobs become automated, we may need to charge a two-thirds or three-quarters automation tax. We're in uncharted waters, and we must have the wisdom to be willing to adapt for the good of society. Remember: this unemployment wave is already on the way because of how unregulated the tech industry has been. We need to start planning for what we do when it hits.

WHAT CAN I DO?

So, how can you help contributionism make the jump from theory to reality? What steps can you take to help shepherd it into existence? Below, I have outlined several actionable things you can do to help. But before getting into those, I want to mention the most important thing you can do: *talk about it*. Tell others about contributionism. We cannot ask for change if we don't know what to ask for, and it is my hope that contributionism can be a solid, concrete "ask."

I mentioned Occupy Wall Street earlier and how it failed because the movement had no concrete requests — contributionism can be that request, but only if people know about it. So, spread it around! Ask your friends about it. Send them this book. Read it as a group. There is strength in numbers. We can either watch the uber-rich flaunt their wealth on social media and wish we were like them, or we can use that same platform to promote contributionism in order to avoid plummeting deeper and deeper into debt slavery while being distracted by the trappings of greed and consumerism.

I can't stress enough that we need to take action now. It has been predicted that if we stay on this course, by 2030, the top 10% of the global population will control *70%* of global wealth — leaving just 30% for the rest of us. Do you really think they'll stop there? Of course not. It *WILL* continue to get worse. Remember: it is the goal of the mega-wealthy to have all of the resources, even if it means none for anyone else.

Will it be a perfectly smooth, easy transition to contributionism? Probably not — large changes always have a few bumps. But now is the easiest it will ever be. Things will only get harder the longer we wait.

Now, on to specific things we can do to make a change. I'll touch on what you can do as a consumer, an employee, and an employer.

CONSUMERS

As a consumer, you vote with your wallet. The number of people out there I've met who complain about our economy yet still turn around and give their money to mega-corporations just for the sake of convenience is staggering. If you want an economy dominated by a few mega-corporations that pay most of their employees terribly — keep on giving them your money. They'll keep doing what they've been doing right along — giving the vast majority of their profits to a handful of extremely wealthy shareholders and executives, siphoning it away from communities. They'll continue to grow and crowd out smaller businesses until they are one of only a few options. Our government will not bust them as monopolies because they own the government.

On the other hand, if you want to see towns populated by small businesses filled with character, with employees working right alongside the business owners and money remaining within the community — vote for it with your wallet by giving those small businesses your money. These independent stores cannot function unless people buy from them. Every time you buy something from a mega-corporation instead of an independent business, that small business is one step closer to having to shut its doors — giving you fewer options and ensuring you must send money out of your community to get what you want. Yes, buying from small local businesses might be a little more expensive. Yes, returns could be more of a hassle. But in the long term, the cost of these small savings and conveniences is less money within your community, fewer options for you to buy from, and fewer places of employment that will pay fair wages.

It doesn't even take all of society being onboard to facilitate this change. If 30% of a mega-corporation's sales dry up, it will be a massive hit to their profits. For some, this may inspire change. For others, it will lead them to cut costs — including jobs. This will be one of the things that big business supporters will latch onto. "These boycotters are hurting American jobs!" they'll cry. When you hear this, remember: working in a factory for $1 a day is technically a job. Yes, people may lose jobs in the short term as companies try to cut costs — but many of these jobs don't pay a living wage. If the people who stopped giving their money to mega-corporations give their money to local and contributionist businesses instead, more of these businesses will be *able* to open because there will be an actual demand for them. As more contributionist companies spring up, the people who were laid off can find better jobs that pay a living wage.

Another important thing to remember: you know how so many grocery stores have laid off most of their cashiers and replaced them with self-checkouts? Has the cost of groceries gone down since then, or has it gone up? Large companies already plan to lay off their workforce as soon as technology makes it possible, and they intend to pocket the money saved. Layoffs will continue to happen even if we don't move to contributionism, which means even less money staying within our communities and more going to yachts for the mega wealthy.

At this point, "supply and demand" is only used for products — what products are in demand and how much/many are available. But what if we also applied this to the way businesses were run? What if we demand ethical conduct from businesses instead of simply products? Suddenly it's no longer just "I need new shoes." It's "I need new shoes from a contributionist company." In this environment, better alternatives can flourish because they're highly in demand — even if there's a mega-corporation next door selling the same products for slightly less.

So, here are some actionable steps you can take to make contributionism a reality. These aren't things you must do all at once; instead, try to take each step as and when you can.

STOP GIVING MEGA-CORPORATIONS YOUR MONEY

This means canceling subscriptions and looking for independent businesses to buy from. I often get some backlash on this, with people making up excuses about how shipping will be less convenient, or prices will be marginally more expensive. All I can think when I hear this is, "How are you so fragile?" For almost all of human existence, fast shipping hasn't existed. Have we really become so soft and spoiled that we can't stand a tiny bit of hassle for a little while in order to improve our lives in the long term? Without taking action, our lives will only get harder and harder. There will never be an easier time than now.

SHOP CONTRIBUTIONIST. IF YOU CAN'T, SHOP LOCAL.

This goes hand-in-hand with not giving your money to mega-corporations. Seek out contributionist companies in your area — many of them will likely advertise as the movement builds steam. By buying from them, you'll keep the money within your community rather than sending most of it off to some rich person living in a mansion hundreds or thousands of miles away. This will also allow contributionist companies to grow and provide more *good* jobs. But do make sure that you check with floor workers to make sure that the company is contributionist and not falsely advertising.

If you don't see contributionist stores yet, or you need something they don't sell, shop at a small local business. Most small businesses are already following contributionist pay practices[86] simply because their profits are leaner compared to mega-corporations.

EMBRACE MINOR INCONVENIENCES

Remember what our ancestors went through. We've been spoiled by instant gratification and ease of living, but in the old days, ordering something could mean a month-long wait or more as it's shipped to you by horse-drawn carriage. This is our generation's fight, and compared to the battles our ancestors fought, it's an easy one. Let's not let them down.

REJECT MATERIALISTIC SHOWS OF WEALTH

Reject luxury brands. Do not simply give respect to people because they bought a fancy watch, and do not define your self-worth by your ability to give money to rich people. To go a step further, consciously make an effort to not be impressed by someone simply because they have money. Remember, the easiest ways to get rich are by having lots of money to start with or by stealing the fruits of your workers' labor.

A person walking around with an expensive designer bag or watch is advertising that they've been fooled into believing it has anything to do with their value. Something inside them makes them feel they need it to be worthy of respect. It isn't their fault — they didn't choose to be born into a materialistic society — but it's important to not validate this belief

---

86 As of early 2023, 86.3% of small business owners made less than $100k each year in income — quite a few of them made far less — putting many of them well within the pay ratio for a company of their size. (See bibliography for citation and more info.) This strangulation of profits comes in large part from consumers giving their business to mega-corporations. By returning our attention to local business, we enable them to continue thriving and to bring their employees with them.

by acting impressed. An eye roll or a gentle scoff is well within "free speech."

EMBRACE SIMPLICITY

and try to live as far beneath your means as possible.

This will provide you with greater stability and help keep you from becoming so desperate that you have no choice but to work for an employer who steals the value of your work. Remember, embracing simplicity isn't about tolerating it because you can't afford anything more, it's about living beneath your means to increase your stability and independence while finding deeper sources of happiness and fulfillment.

DIFFERENTIATE BETWEEN WANTS AND NEEDS

Try to become the sort of person who finds contentment without having to buy it. Focus on attaining your needs and reducing your wants to things you don't need to subscribe to or pay a ton for. Incidentally, these free or low-cost pleasures are usually the things that bring the most fulfillment.

BE PROUD AND VISIBLE

Humans are pack animals. We have a built-in desire to fit into the pack. By making it known that you're a contributionist, you help pull more people to the cause. Be proud — the fight to have people's time valued is a noble one.

MAKE A CONSCIOUS EFFORT TO BREAK YOUR PROGRAMMING

We have all been born and raised in a society that bombards you with the message "fancy products and money = personal value." A lifetime of immersion in this programming won't undo itself on its own — we must make a conscious effort. Internal mantras can be helpful for this. Come up with what works for you, but here are a couple of examples to get you started.

> When slick, flashy advertisements or celebrity or influencer endorsements slide into your social media feed, intentionally think to yourself, "They're trying to manipulate me into thinking my life is missing something so they can take my money."

> When you see a person walking down the street in designer clothes, think to yourself, "Wow. Someone who tries so hard to appear fancy must really rely on accumulation to feel self-worth."

TELL THE PEOPLE WHAT YOU WANT

Advertise things that you want to buy that aren't available in your area except from mega-corporations. This is necessary so that entrepreneurs willing to start contributionist companies can better see what is in demand. By being open about what you need, contributionist entrepreneurs will be better able to target areas of demand, allowing them to start businesses with less risk and providing you with more alternatives to buying from mega-corporations.

REMEMBER THAT THIS IS AN ACTIVE CHOICE

The ultra-rich have been working hard for many years to consolidate power and resources as much as they can. This isn't something that can just change without making an active choice. It will take slightly more effort to shop local. It will be slightly less convenient to shop for clothes in person or risk an annoying returns process. This is a choice we must continue to make, not just as an "every once-in-a-while thing," but whenever possible. When you need to go for a coffee, or a sandwich, or some clothes, or a book, and you feel yourself falling into the pattern of buying it from a huge corporation — just make a habit of remembering "*or* I could get it from a cool local store."

AS AN EMPLOYEE

SHARE CONTRIBUTIONISM WITH FELLOW EMPLOYEES

Remember, if your boss discourages this, it's because they think contributionism might work. Preventing worker communication is NEVER in the worker's best interest. Obviously, the people squeezing work from you for as little money as possible will come up with excuses about why you shouldn't organize or ask for more — because it hurts their bottom line when you come together.

ADVOCATE FOR TRANSPARENCY

When you have a good number of employees onboard, ask your employer to be transparent with income, costs, profits, and pay. Remember that people lie — demand transparency. After all, by not discussing pay, who benefits? Only the people keeping all the money.

SEEK OTHER WORK

If your employer refuses to give in to the reasonable request of transparency, begin looking for other work at a contributionist company or small businesses.

CONSIDER STARTING YOUR OWN BUSINESS

If you and enough other employees are contributionist, and your company refuses to change, consider starting your own contributionist store in the same area. Remember, the consumers following this philosophy will be actively looking for contributionist stores in their area. This is fertile ground for new business ventures. See the "As an Entrepreneur" section below.

AS A SMALL BUSINESS OWNER OR EMPLOYER

As I said before, many small businesses are already "informally contributionist."[87] For you, this could be the start of your golden age.

MAKE IT OFFICIAL

Make sure your employees understand what contributionism is, and state that your business will be contributionist. Follow the requirements laid out in the next section.

---

87 I already mentioned the percentage of small businesses making more than $100k/year. The *average* earning of a small business owner is $72,298/year, according to PayScale. For a company with 10–24 employees who are paid at least $12.05/hr, this is already in line with contributionist pay ratios. See bibliography for more data.

BE TRANSPARENT

First, be transparent with income, costs, profits, and pay. Make the numbers available to your employees, or a representative they choose. Show them that you recognize their time and effort by not hiding the results of their labor from them. I go into more details below in the "Requirements to Be a Contributionist Business" section.

ADVERTISE AND SPREAD THE WORD

Advertise the fact that you're a contributionist company. This will attract business from contributionist consumers, and it will attract workers who are trying to leave exploitative companies. Spread the idea of contributionism as well — as consumers change their buying habits, they will begin buying from you. Each person you get onboard can be another local shopper.

DO BUSINESS WITH CONTRIBUTIONIST SUPPLIERS

When possible, seek out suppliers who also abide by contributionist principles. In the short term, this may mean a slight price increase, but in the long term, it will mean more options for you to choose from.

AS AN ENTREPRENEUR

As contributionism builds momentum, demand for products from small businesses and contributionist companies will grow, creating new opportunities for entrepreneurs. Now is the time to act!

LOOK FOR AREAS OF OPPORTUNITY TO START A CONTRIBUTIONIST COMPANY

The law of supply and demand is foundational to business. Right now, there is low demand for products from small businesses, as so many consumers give their money to mega-corporations instead. This means high risk for starting a new business since you must compete with stores that have far greater resources and reach. As more people jump aboard the cause, this will begin to change. Where before you would have had to compete with huge corporate department stores and delivery companies, you may find yourself the only contributionist option in an area full of contributionist consumers.

ADVERTISE THAT YOU'RE HIRING

Many people working for companies that refuse to adopt contributionism will be seeking better employment. Play it right, and you can staff your business with a workforce that is already experienced in the field.

REQUIREMENTS TO BE A CONTRIBUTIONIST BUSINESS

For those business owners who want to pursue contributionist policies, I want to easily lay out right here what must be done to achieve this.

1. **Transparency.** The foundation required for contributionism to work. Workers nominate three representatives who meet with the business owner to go over financial info. These meetings are recorded and made available to the rest of the workers. On a monthly basis, the boss sits down and goes over financial information with them, including expenditures, revenues, profits, pay rates, and reinvestment plans for the profits, as well as the status of investor payouts if applicable. This includes going over bank statements, accounting information, and expense reports. These representatives then brief workers on what they've learned so that the workers of the business understand exactly what is going on.

2. **Investment.** Many businesses need startup funds to begin, and those funds are often gained from investors. Ensure that your investment terms state that the investor will be bought out at no higher than a 300% ROI. This allows you to retain ownership of your company and to distribute profits back to yourself and your workers.

3. **Pay ratios.** Ensure you follow contributionist pay ratios for your size of business, both for wages and for profit-sharing.

BIBLIOGRAPHY

"A well-informed citizenry is the best defense against tyranny."

— Thomas Jefferson

Thanks for stopping by the bibliography! I applaud you for not taking claims at face value.

This bibliography was something I decided to include partway through the process of writing the book. I debated leaving it out so that it wouldn't be rooted in one time and place, but I think showing that there is significant evidence behind the things I'm saying is important, even if it is just a snapshot of how things were at the time it was written. Misinformation is how those with power keep people voting against their own interests — and the best way to fight misinformation is with knowledge.

In determining the best way to present this information, I decided to embrace the digital era that we live in. I've cited names of studies and articles, as well as included links so that you can read and examine them for yourself. As with the rest of this book, accessibility is the name of the game for me. While many of these references point straight to studies or scholarly articles, those can get a bit dense for some readers. I've also included more accessible articles that interpret data in plain English or that simply provide more info on a specific subject.

I recognize that this will be much easier for people reading the e-book version than a physical copy, but for those going old-school with their reading, a Google search for the title and authors should bring you to the correct page.

Also, keep in mind, the internet is a shifting space. It's like having access to a vast library, but the books are constantly popping in and out of existence. Some of the linked websites may go down, or URLs might change, resulting in a broken link. They may also be taken down by those who own the businesses running the websites. I hope this doesn't happen, and it's one reason I hesitated to add this section, but it's the cost of using the internet to provide extra information. I have compiled an archive of these sources, with the webpage or study turned into a PDF document so that they can remain available even if the links stop working or the host sites go down. I plan to make these available on my personal website, economicdecency.org. Hopefully, this ends up being a waste of time. If nothing else, it could always be an easy way to cross-reference if you're reading a physical copy of the book.

When you're looking through these entries, know that anything in *italics* is my comment. I've included a couple of graphs, but I realized quickly that including all the relevant graphs would make this bibliography longer than the rest of the book. If you find visual representations helpful, many of the linked pages do include them!

PART 1: THE PHILOSOPHY

1: Mujica, A., Crowell, C., Villano, M., & Uddin, K. (2022). ADDICTION BY DESIGN: Some Dimensions and Challenges of Excessive Social Media Use. *Medical Research Archives, 10*(2). doi:10.18103/mra.v10i2.2677 (https://esmed.org/MRA/mra/article/view/2677)

2: *One earner means one person paying for the couple ($76,486/yr)* PLUS paying to raise a child (~$13,000/yr)**. That's $89,486 a year required, and the average single income is $59,987/yr.****

- *Cost per year to live as a couple: $76,468/yr* — Sheridan, P. InCharge Debt Solutions. (2024). Average Monthly Expenses for American Households. (https://www.incharge.org/financial-literacy/budgeting-saving/average-monthly-expenses/)
- **Cost to raise a child: $12,350–13,900/yr* — U.S. Department of Agriculture, Center for Nutrition Policy and Promotion. (2017). Expenditures on Children by Families, 2015. Number adjusted for inflation. (https://www.fns.usda.gov/cnpp/2015-expenditures-children-families)
- ***Average income: $59,987/yr* — U.S. Department of Justice. (2023). Means Testing - Census Bureau, IRS Data and Administrative Expenses Multipliers. (https://www.justice.gov/ust/eo/bapcpa/20220401/bci_data/median_income_table.htm)

3. Galicza, N. (2024, October 19). Who owns the news? Deseret Magazine. (https://www.deseret.com/magazine/2024/10/19/who-owns-newspapers-tv-news/)

4: *Trickle-down economics has actually halved our country's economic growth, dropping it from 2.8% yearly in the '60s and '70s to 1.4% yearly from the '80s to present day.**
- *How trickle-down economics works* — Kenton, W. (2024). Trickle-Down Economics: Theory, Policies, and Critique. Investopedia. (https://www.investopedia.com/terms/t/trickledowntheory.asp)
- **The results of trickle-down economics* — Lichtblau, M. (2019). The Fallacy and Persistence of "Trickle-Down Economics". *Brown Political Review.* (https://brownpoliticalreview.org/the-fallacy-and-persistence-of-trickle-down-economics/)

FIGURE 1

The trickle-down experiment has failed

Annual cash market income growth of all tax units and the bottom 90 percent of tax units across business cycles

Note: Business cycles were constructed from peak to peak through author's analysis using the National Bureau of Economic Research's business cycle dates. The short peak-to-peak period between 1980 and 1981 is grouped with the previous 1973–1980 peak-to-peak period. 2014 was the last year in the current period for which data were available and is not itself a business cycle peak.

Sources: Author's analysis of the cash market income of tax units using National Bureau of Economic Research, "U.S. Business Cycle Expansions and Contractions," available at http://www.nber.org/cycles.html (last accessed June 2015); Emmanuel Saez and Thomas Piketty, "Income Inequality in the United States, 1913-1998," *The Quarterly Journal of Economics*, 118 (1) (2003): 1–39, available at http://eml.berkeley.edu/~saez/.

Sourced from AmericanProgress.org

6: *A few examples of politicians prioritizing businesses over the people:*

- *This article goes into "political economics" and gives us an example using sugar industry subsidies, a policy which costs consumers an estimated $2-3 billion per year* — Frieden, J. (2020). The Political Economy of Economic Policy. *Finance & Development*, 57(2), 4–9. International Monetary Fund. (https://www.imf.org/en/Publications/fandd/issues/2020/06/political-economy-of-economic-policy-jeff-frieden)

- *Article that discusses campaign finance and how money given by companies to politicians results in massive payouts from the government to those companies — including corporate bailouts funded by American taxpayers* — Allison, B., & Harkins, S. (2014, November 17). Fixed Fortunes: Biggest corporate political interests spend billions, get trillions. Sunlight Foundation. (https://sunlightfoundation.com/2014/11/17/fixed-fortunes-biggest-corporate-political-interests-spend-billions-get-trillions/)

- *Article about politicians who receive funding from big oil companies resisting carbon pricing and other sustainability attempts, in spite of recommendations from the American Petroleum Institute* — Cama, T., Sobczyk, N. (2021, March 26). Conservatives, greens snub Big Oil's carbon price play. *E&E News*. (https://www.eenews.net/articles/conservatives-greens-snub-big-oils-carbon-price-play/)
  - *How do politicians get away with this? A Harvard Gazette article on how intentional misinformation about climate change is used to influence public policy* — Powell, A., Supran, G., & Oreskes, N. (2017, 2021). Assessing ExxonMobil's climate change communications (1977 — 2014). *Environmental Research Letters*, *12*(8), 084019 (https://news.harvard.edu/gazette/story/2021/09/oil-companies-discourage-climate-action-study-says/)
  - *Another source on big oil companies "greenwashing" their intentions. From a Democratic source, but the article is a summary of findings from the Congressional Subcommittee on Environment and includes links directly to the source information. The Congressional Report itself is also linked* — U.S. House Committee on Oversight and Reform. (2022, December 9). Oversight Committee Releases New Documents Showing Big Oil's Greenwashing Campaign and Failure to Reduce Emissions. (https://oversightdemocrats.house.gov/news/press-releases/oversight-committee-releases-new-documents-showing-big-oil-s-greenwashing)
  - *Congressional report* — Maloney, C., Khanna, R. (2022) (https://oversightdemocrats.house.gov/sites/evo-subsites/democrats-oversight.house.gov/files/2022-12-09.COR_Supplemental_Memo-

Fossil_Fuel_Industry_Disinformation.pdf)

7: Carey, R.. Unbiased. (2025). How much income puts you in the top 1%, 5%, or 10%? Retrieved from Unbiased.com. (https://www.unbiased.com/discover/banking/how-much-income-puts-you-in-the-top-1-5-or-10)

8: Kent, A., Ricketts, L. Institute for Economic Equity. (2024). The State of U.S. Wealth Inequality. St. Louis Fed. (https://www.stlouisfed.org/institute-for-economic-equity/the-state-of-us-wealth-inequality)

9: Graph from Statista — Statista. (2024) Wealth distribution in the U.S.

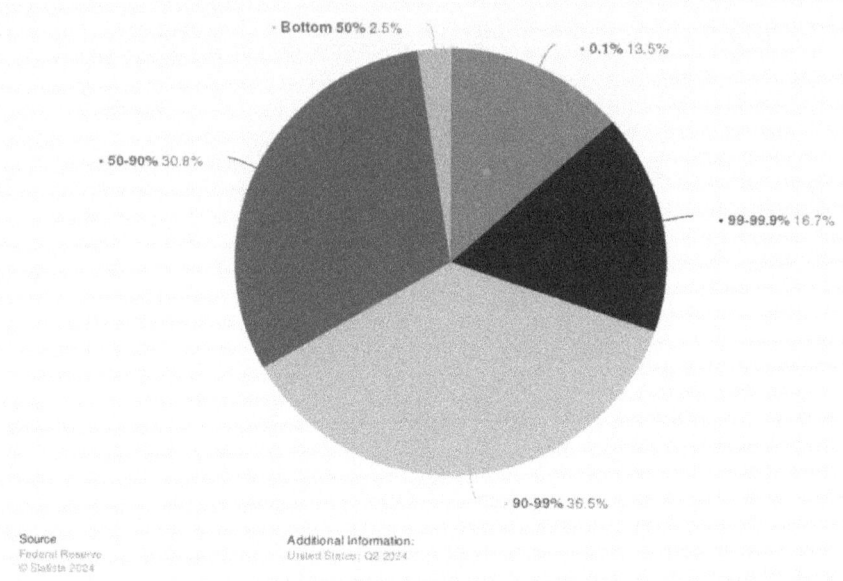

Wealth distribution in the United States in the second quarter of 2024

(https://www.statista.com/statistics/203961/wealth-distribution-for-the-us/)

10: Landy, B. (2012). Corporate profits rise to new heights as wages decline. The Century Foundation. (https://tcf.org/content/commentary/graph-corporate-profits-rise-to-new-heights-as-wages-decline/)

11: Bivens, J., & Kandra, J. (2023) CEO pay remains near historically high levels: CEO-to-worker compensation ratio was 344-to-1 in 2022. Economic Policy Institute. (https://www.epi.org/publication/ceo-pay-in-2022/)

12: Economic Policy Institute. (2024). The Productivity — Pay Gap. (https://www.epi.org/productivity-pay-gap/)

13: *A table including average weekly worker pay throughout the years* — U.S. Bureau of Labor Statistics. (2009). Women in the Labor Force: A Databook (2009 Edition). Table 16. Median usual weekly earnings of full-time wage and salary workers, by race, Hispanic or Latino ethnicity, and sex, 1979-2008 annual averages. (https://www.bls.gov/cps/wlftable16.htm)

14: *Sourced from the National Association of Realtors* — YCharts. (2024). US Existing Home Median Sales Price. (https://ycharts.com/indicators/us_existing_home_median_sales_price)

15: Prysmakova, P. (2024). Work Motivation under Communist Rule: Heritage from the Past in Modern Public Sector Organisations. *Central European Economic Journal, 11*(58), 269–285. (https://sciendo.com/article/10.2478/ceej-2024-0018)

16: Gale, W., & Vignaux, S. (2023). The difference in how the wealthy make money—and pay taxes. Brookings Institution. (https://www.brookings.edu/articles/the-difference-in-how-the-wealthy-make-money-and-pay-taxes/)

17: Americans for Tax Fairness. (2024). Engine of Inequality: A Flood of Corporate Profits Is Enriching Wealthy Shareholders Through Stock Buybacks and Dividends, At The Expense of Workers and The Public. (https://americansfortaxfairness.org/wp-content/uploads/Dividends-and-Buybacks-Report.pdf)

18: PolicyLink. (2024). Overview of America's Working Poor. (https://www.policylink.org/data-in-action/overview-america-working-poor)

19: Government Accountability Office. (2020). Millions of Full-Time Workers Rely on Federal Health Care and Food Assistance Programs.

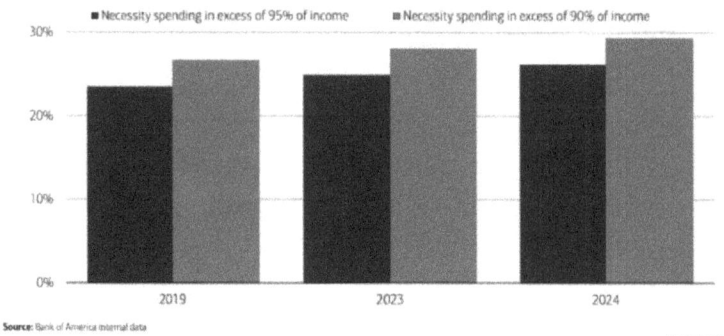

Exhibit 2: 26% of households are living 'paycheck to paycheck' in the sense that their necessity spending is close to their total household income
Proportion of households where necessity spending exceeds 95% and 90% of their household income (%)

Source: Bank of America internal data

BANK OF AMERICA INSTITUTE

"Blue" indicates the percentage of households that spend more than 95% of their income, and "red" indicates the percentage of households that spend more than 90% of their income on "essentials for life."

Bank of America Institute

(https://www.gao.gov/products/gao-21-45)

20.
Bank of America Institute. (2024). Paycheck to Paycheck: Lower-Income Households.
 (https://institute.bankofamerica.com/content/dam/economic-insights/paycheck-to-paycheck-lower-income-households.pdf)

22: HRZone. (n.d.). What is Corporate Personhood? Corporate Personhood definition. (https://hrzone.com/glossary/what-is-corporate-personhood/)

23: Ladegaard Law. (n.d.). Limited Liability: The Corporate Shield Doctrine. (http://www.ladegaardlaw.com/blog/limited-liability-the-corporate-shield-doctrine)

24: RocketLawyer. (n.d.). Corporations Are People? The Origins of Corporate Personhood. (https://www.rocketlawyer.com/business-and-contracts/legal-guide/corporations-people-origins-corporate-personhood)

25: Torres-Spelliscy, C. (2017). Does "We the People" include corporations? American Bar Association. (https://www.americanbar.org/groups/crsj/publications/human_rights_magazine_home/we-the-people/we-the-people-corporations/)

26: *The impact of the Citizens United vs FEC ruling* — OpenSecrets.org. (2019, January). "Nine Years After Citizens United, Campaign Finance Landscape Transformed." (https://www.opensecrets.org/news/2019/01/citizens-united/) *Even more info, including info on private mega-wealthy donors* — OpenSecrets.org. (2020, January 14). "A Decade Under Citizens United." (https://www.opensecrets.org/news/reports/a-decade-under-citizens-united)

27: Soper, K. (2017). A New Hedonism: A Post-Consumerism Vision. The Next System Project. (https://thenextsystem.org/learn/stories/new-hedonism-post-consumerism-vision)

28: Enifeni, F. (2023). The Pursuit of Happiness is a Battle Against Capitalism. *MediaCat Magazine.* (https://mediacatmagazine.co.uk/the-pursuit-of-happiness-is-a-battle-against-capitalism/)

29: *Especially note the "Creation of Moral Hazard and Too-Big-to-Fail Competitive Advantage" section* — Scott, H. S. (n.d.). Criticisms of Bailouts Generally. COVID-19 and Economics. MIT Press. (https://covid-19.mitpress.mit.edu/pub/vf54oo8p/release/1)

30: Public Citizen. (2021, April 26). Corporations that Received Billions During the Pandemic Cut Thousands of Workers While Paying

CEOs Millions. (https://www.citizen.org/news/corporations-that-received-billions-during-the-pandemic-laid-off-thousands-of-workers-and-gave-ceos-millions/)
Some specifics — Public Citizen. (2021). The COVID-19 Corporate Hall of Shame. (https://www.citizen.org/article/the-covid-19-corporate-hall-of-shame/)

31: *Poor homeownership rates, especially for people under 35* — National Association of Home Builders. (2024, August). Lowest Homeownership Rate in Four Years. (https://www.nahb.org/blog/2024/08/lowest-homeownership-rate-in-four-years)
Increasing rental as mortgage payments skyrocket — Maister, P. (2024, August 6). Renter Households Growing Three Times Faster Than Homeowner Households. GlobeSt. (https://www.globest.com/2024/08/06/renter-households-growing-three-times-faster-than-homeowner-households/)

32: Bankrate. (2024, July 15). More Than A Third of Workers Say They're Living Paycheck To Paycheck. (https://www.bankrate.com/banking/living-paycheck-to-paycheck-survey/)

33: Federal Reserve Board. (2024, May 21). Economic Well-Being of U.S. Households in 2023. (https://www.federalreserve.gov/newsevents/pressreleases/other20240521a.htm)

34: *Article* — Kotkin, J. (2022, January). Our Neo-Feudal Future. First Things. (https://www.firstthings.com/article/2022/01/our-neo-feudal-future)
Book — Kotkin, J. (2020). *The Coming of Neo-Feudalism: A Warning to the Global Middle Class.* Encounter Books. https://joelkotkin.com/books/

36: Parkinson's NSW. (n.d.). Four Happy Hormones: Understanding Dopamine, Serotonin, Oxytocin, and Endorphins. Retrieved from (https://www.parkinsonsnsw.org.au/four-happy-hormones/)

37: Ducharme, J. (2022, November 29). The Science Behind Why Shopping Is So Addictive. *TIME*. (https://time.com/6235522/why-shopping-is-addictive/)
This one is pretty dark actually. It discusses how shopping can spike dopamine and how companies consciously use that to drive sales. They're actually calling it "neuromarketing." A more accurate description is "consciously manipulating people's brain chemistry to convince them they have to give you their money." It pitches two strategies: get people addicted or get them scared. Really, do give this a read, and consider it from an ethical standpoint — Pathmonk. (n.d.). From Dopamine to Dollars: Exploring the Neurological Roots of Consumer Behavior. (https://pathmonk.com/exploring-the-neurological-roots-of-consumer-behavior/)

38: Northstar Behavioral Health. (n.d.). Is It Possible to Be Addicted to Spending Money? (https://www.northstarbehavioralhealthmn.com/resources/is-it-possible-to-be-addicted-to-spending-money) Gregory, H. (2023). Wealth Addiction: The New Affliction of the Upper Class. Sarah Lawrence College. (https://digitalcommons.slc.edu/undergrad_selectedworks/16/)

39: Calipari, E. S., Siciliano, C. A., Zimmer, B. A., & Jones, S. R. (2016). Cocaine Self-Administration Produces Long-Lasting Alterations in Dopamine Transporter Responses to Cocaine. *The Journal of Neuroscience, 36*(30), 7807–7816. (https://www.jneurosci.org/content/36/30/7807)

40: "The mutual-aid tendency in man has so remote an origin, and is so deeply interwoven with all the past evolution of the human race, that it

has been maintained by mankind up to the present time, notwithstanding all vicissitudes of history." —— Kropotkin, P. (1902). *Mutual Aid: A Factor of Evolution.*
Article on the topic — Raghavan, M. (2022). Putting Kropotkin Back into the Concept of Mutual Aid. *Science for the People, 24*(3), 7–10. (https://magazine.scienceforthepeople.org/vol24-3-cooperation/putting-kropotkin-back-into-the-concept-of-mutual-aid/)

45: Ravichandran, S. (n.d.). The Dark Side of Venture Capital: How VCs Can Destroy Companies. LinkedIn. (https://www.linkedin.com/pulse/dark-side-venture-capital-how-vcs-can-destroy-swarup-ravichandran/)
Private Equity List. (n.d.). The Dark Side of Venture Capital: Why It's Bad. https://blog.privateequitylist.com/the-dark-side-of-venture-capital-why-its-bad/

47: U.S. Government Accountability Office. (2020). Wage-Earning Adults: Characteristics of Medicaid Enrollees and SNAP Recipients. GAO-21-45. (https://www.gao.gov/products/gao-21-45)

48: Seligman, M. E. P., & Maier, S. F. (1967). Failure to escape traumatic shock. *Journal of Experimental Psychology, 74*(1), 1–9. (https://ppc.sas.upenn.edu/sites/default/files/lhtheoryevidence.pdf)

49: *Wage increase leads to more people taking jobs* — Emanuel, N., & Harrington, E. (2020). Elasticities of Productivity and Labor Supply with Respect to Wages. Job Market Paper, Harvard University. (https://scholar.harvard.edu/files/nataliaemanuel/files/emanuel_jmp.pdf)
Furman, J. (2023, January 24). Higher wages for low-income workers lead to higher productivity. Peterson Institute for International Economics. (https://www.piie.com/blogs/realtime-economic-issues-watch/higher-wages-low-income-workers-lead-higher-productivity)

Child labor to get around raising wages — Economic Policy Institute. (2023, March 14). Child labor laws are under attack in states across the country. (https://www.epi.org/publication/child-labor-laws-under-attack/)

The Conversation. (2023, June 26). States Are Loosening Child Labor Laws. *U.S. News & World Report*. (https://www.usnews.com/news/best-states/articles/2023-06-26/states-are-loosening-child-labor-laws)

Prisoner leasing to get around raising wages — Weinstein, L. (2021, June 16). The Convict Leasing System. Inside Adams: Science, Technology & Business. Library of Congress. (https://blogs.loc.gov/inside_adams/2021/06/convict-leasing-system/)

Richter, F. (2024, January 5). Prisoners Earn Cents Per Hour for Labor in U.S. Prisons. *Statista*. (https://www.statista.com/chart/32814/mean-hourly-wage-of-prisoners-in-state-facilities-working-regular-prison-jobs-by-state/)

50: *Trends in number of working parents since the late 1960s*

Fox, L., Han, W.J., Ruhm, C., Waldfogel, J. Time for children: trends in the employment patterns of parents, 1967-2009. *Demography*. February 2013, *50*(1): 25–49. doi: 10.1007/s13524-012-0138-4. PMID: 22990610; PMCID: PMC9206509. (https://pmc.ncbi.nlm.nih.gov/articles/PMC9206509/)

51: *CEOs and investors soaking up the profits instead of workers* — Mishel, L., & Kandra, J. (2021). CEO Pay in 2020. Economic Policy Institute. (https://www.epi.org/publication/ceo-pay-in-2020/)

The result of these stagnating wages. — Joshi, P., Walters, A., Shafer, L., Diversity Data Kids. (2022). Full-Time Work Alone Won't Close the Child Opportunity Gap.
(https://www.diversitydatakids.org/research-library/blog/full-time-work-alone-wont-close-child-opportunity-gap)
A detailed overview of what this does to children in working families who are still struggling financially — United for ALICE. (n.d.). The Consequences of Insufficient Household Income.
(https://www.unitedforalice.org/consequences)

52: Luona Lin, L., Parker, K., Horowitz, JM. Pew Research Center. (2024). Teachers' views of parent involvement.
(https://www.pewresearch.org/social-trends/2024/04/04/teachers-views-of-parent-involvement/)

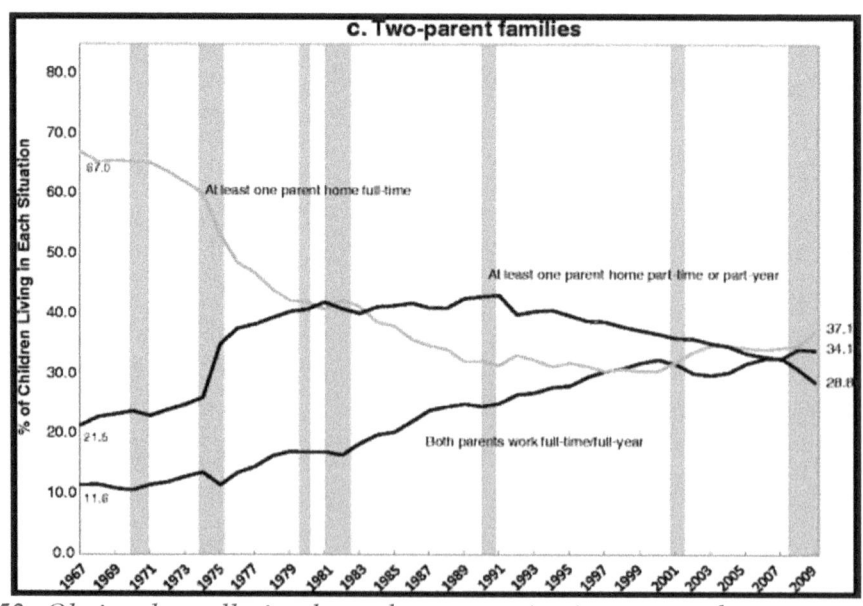

53: *Obviously, pollution has a huge negative impact on the environment. It's hard not to hear about it these days. But let's say you really don't even care about the ecosystem. Or that you don't believe in*

"climate change." Let's just focus on pollution's direct impact on the human body. Your body.
Air pollution — European Environment Agency. (2024). How Air Pollution Affects Our Health. (https://www.eea.europa.eu/en/topics/in-depth/air-pollution/eow-it-affects-our-health)
Water pollution study — Xu, X., Lin, L., & Yang, H. (2022). Effects of Water Pollution on Human Health and Disease Heterogeneity: A Review. *Frontiers in Environmental Science, 10*, 880246. doi:10.3389/fenvs.2022.880246. (https://www.frontiersin.org/journals/environmental-science/articles/10.3389/fenvs.2022.880246/full)
Soil and water pollution study briefing for Cardiologists — Münzel, T, Hahad, O, Daiber, A., Landrigan, P. J. Soil and water pollution and human health: what should cardiologists worry about? *Cardiovascular Research.* March 31, 2023, *119*(2): 440–449. doi: 10.1093/cvr/cvac082. PMID: 35772469; PMCID: PMC10064841. (https://pmc.ncbi.nlm.nih.gov/articles/PMC10064841/)

54: *Market manipulation breakdown* — Tycko & Zavareei Whistleblower Practice Group of Tycko & Zavareei LLP (2024). What is Market Manipulation?. *The National Law Review.* (https://natlawreview.com/article/what-market-manipulation#google_vignette)
Examples — Gibbs Law Group. (n.d.). Market Manipulation Examples. (https://www.classlawgroup.com/securities-fraud/stock/market-manipulation/examples)
In his book, A Random Walk Down Wall Street, Princeton University professor Burton Malkiel claimed that "a blindfolded monkey throwing darts at a newspaper's financial pages could select a portfolio that would do just as well as one carefully selected by experts." This famous claim was tested in the linked study, which found that simulated "monkey portfolios" did as well or better than the market or cap-weighted portfolios. — Arnott, R. D., Hsu, J., Kalesnik, V., & Tindall, P. (2013). The Surprising Alpha from Malkiel's Monkey and Upside-

Down Strategies. Research Affiliates.
(https://www.researchaffiliates.com/content/dam/ra/publications/pdf/96
2-surprising-alpha-from-malkiels-monkey.pdf)

55: *How stock trading impacts retirements. Article from 2009, just after the crash.* — Urban Institute. Butrica, B., Smith, K., & Toder, E. (2009). Retirement Security and the Stock Market Crash: What Are the Possible Outcomes?
(https://www.urban.org/sites/default/files/publication/30811/411998-
Retirement-Security-and-the-Stock-Market-Crash-What-Are-the-
Possible-Outcomes-.PDF)

56: *This study estimates the average human generation interval as 26.9 years. Using this information, we can estimate the number of generations: 250,000 years ÷ 26.9 years per generation ≈ 9,294 generations. This study is slightly debated, (usually with higher numbers of generations) but I feel that my "2,000 generations" number is more than safe.* — Wang, R.J., Al-Saffar, S.I., Rogers, J, Hahn, M.W. Human generation times across the past 250,000 years. *Science Advances,* January 6, 2023, 9(1):eabm7047. doi: 10.1126/sciadv.abm7047. PMID: 36608127; PMCID: PMC9821931. (https://pmc.ncbi.nlm.nih.gov/articles/PMC9821931/)

57: *An article on the Xia dynasty, the first ancient Chinese Dynasty. This one is so far back that many details are uncertain* — Gotter, A. (2021, October 16). Xia Dynasty: The First of the Ancient Chinese Dynasties. TheCollector. (https://www.thecollector.com/xia-dynasty-
first-ancient-chinese-dynasty/)
The Shang Dynasty succeeded the Xia Dynasty. This one is more recent and much more well-recorded — Encyclopaedia Britannica. (2024, November 5). Zhou. (https://www.britannica.com/biography/Zhou)

59: Alexander, L. & Moore, M. (2024, December 11). "Deontological Ethics." Stanford Encyclopedia of Philosophy. (https://plato.stanford.edu/entries/ethics-deontological/)

60: CNBC. (2024, May 14). Problems that rich people face, according to therapists. (https://www.cnbc.com/2024/05/14/problems-that-rich-people-face-according-to-therapists-.html)
Gotter, A., & Legg, T. J. (2023, August 16). How Anxiety Affects Your Body. Healthline. (https://www.healthline.com/health/anxiety/effects-on-body)

61: PYMNTS Intelligence. (2024). New Reality Check: The Paycheck-to-Paycheck Report: Why One-Third of High Earners Live Paycheck to Paycheck. PYMNTS.com. (https://www.pymnts.com/study/new-reality-check-paycheck-to-paycheck-high-income-consumer-finance/)

62: Energy Education. Anthropogenic. (https://energyeducation.ca/encyclopedia/Anthropogenic)

63: a) The Case Solutions. (n.d.). Ben & Jerry Ice Cream Company Harvard Case Solution & Analysis. (https://www.thecasesolutions.com/ben-jerry-ice-cream-company-22911)
b) *This article (from Money Watch) is a response to Ben and Jerry's (who were owned by Unilever at the time) endorsement of Occupy Wall Street. That's its own debate — the reason I'm including this article is to point out that the wage cap increasing and then vanishing was not the result of financial stress or changing beliefs in how employees should be treated. Rather, it was the result of being unable to find replacement CEOs willing to limit their own income based on employee income. This is a greed issue, not a pay ratio issue.* — Edwards, J. (2011). Occupy Wall Street: Why Ben & Jerry's Endorsement Rings Hollow. CBS News. (https://www.cbsnews.com/news/occupy-wall-street-why-ben-jerrys-endorsement-rings-hollow/)

175

64: a) Fortune. (2021). 100 Best Companies to Work For.
(https://fortune.com/ranking/best-companies/)
b) Craft.co. (2021). W. L. Gore & Associates Financials.
(https://craft.co/w-l-gore-associates/financials)
c) Marshall, B. (2024). The Unconventional Success of W.L. Gore &
Associates. FlowchainSensei.
(https://flowchainsensei.wordpress.com/2024/01/14/the-
unconventional-success-of-w-l-gore-associates/)
d) W. L. Gore & Associates. (n.d.). Our Story - History and
Information (https://www.gore.com/about/the-gore-story)

65: a) Pereira, D. Business Model Analyst. (2023). Is Patagonia
Profitable? (https://businessmodelanalyst.com/is-patagonia-
profitable/#Timeline_of_Patagonia_Financial_Growth_and_Funding)
b) Ardill, L. (2023). Patagonia's Culture: Values and Low Turnover
Success. Workvivo. (https://www.workvivo.com/blog/patagonia-
values-culture-turnover/)

66: Graziosi, G. (2021). CEO who Fox News called 'socialist' for $70k
minimum wage says Rush Limbaugh hoped for his failure. *The
Independent.*
(https://www.independent.co.uk/news/world/americas/dan-price-
gravity-fox-news-b1831429.html)
*And here's what has actually happened: Harvard Business School is
using Gravity Payments as a success story of how compensation fosters
productivity* — Wheeler, M. (2018). Three years ago, this boss set a
$70,000 minimum wage for his employees—and the move is still
paying off. Harvard Business School Online.
(https://online.hbs.edu/blog/post/three-years-ago-this-boss-set-a-usd70-
000-minimum-wage-for-his-employees-and-the-move-is-still-paying-
off)

68: *So far, an estimated 36 million people have lost their jobs due to automation. And projections indicate that's just the start* — TechJury. (2025, January 24). 17 Jobs Lost to Automation Statistics [2025]: AI Job Displacement. (https://techjury.net/blog/jobs-lost-to-automation-statistics/)

69: Ranked Choice Voting Resource Center. (n.d.). What is Ranked Choice Voting (RCV)? (https://www.rcvresources.org/what-is-rcv/) Athens Politics Nerd. (2023, December 12). ACC Commission urges state legislature to allow ranked-choice voting. (https://athenspoliticsnerd.com/acc-commission-urges-state-legislature-to-allow-ranked-choice-voting/)

PART 2: THE NITTY-GRITTY

70: *This image is hard to see, but it's an important reminder provided by history. This man is looking at his five-year-old daughter's hand and foot because his village did not produce enough rubber to meet the quota. These quotas were imposed by privately owned rubber manufacturing companies, with the largest being the Abir Congo Company. When corporations don't see people as people, but rather tools to make them more money, they become very capable and willing to do horrific things to maximize profit and productivity. This is what happens. We know it because we've seen it. This example isn't particularly old — it largely took place from 1885 to1908. And it's only one example — it only takes a few minutes of searching to find countless more.*
More information on private companies savaging the Congo during this period

BBC News. (2020, June 12). Leopold II: Belgium 'wakes up' to its bloody colonial past. (https://www.bbc.com/news/world-europe-53017188)

73: a) U.S. Department of Health and Human Services, Office of the Assistant Secretary for Planning and Evaluation. (2024). National Uninsured Rate at 8.2 Percent in the First Quarter of 2024. (https://aspe.hhs.gov/sites/default/files/documents/ee0475e44e27daef00 155e95a24fd023/nhis-q1-2024-datapoint.pdf)
b) Tolbert, J., Drake, P., & Damico, A. Kaiser Family Foundation (KFF). (2023). Key Facts about the Uninsured Population. (https://www.kff.org/uninsured/issue-brief/key-facts-about-the-uninsured-population/)

74: Mayo Clinic. (n.d.). Executive Health Program overview. Mayo Clinic. (https://www.mayoclinic.org/departments-centers/mayo-clinic-executive-health-program/sections/overview/ovc-20253196)
Mayo Clinic. (n.d.). What to expect from the Executive Health Program. Mayo Clinic. (https://www.mayoclinic.org/departments-centers/mayo-clinic-executive-health-program/sections/what-to-expect/gnc-20253339)

75: Blümel, M. & Busse, R., Technische Universität Berlin. Commonwealth Fund. (2020). Germany: Health System Summary. (https://www.commonwealthfund.org/international-health-policy-center/countries/germany)
Australian Government Department of Health. (2023). Overview of the Australian Health System. (https://www.health.gov.au/about-us/the-australian-health-system)

76: CNN. (2024, September 19). US ranks last on key health care measures compared with other high-income nations, Commonwealth report finds. (https://www.cnn.com/2024/09/19/health/health-care-rankings-high-income-nations-commonwealth-report/index.html)

77: George, S. Bankrate. (2024). Average business loan interest rates in 2024. (https://www.bankrate.com/loans/small-business/average-business-loan-rates/)

78: *General summary* — Cynomi. (n.d.). 7 Risk Assessment Methods to Streamline Risk Management. (https://cynomi.com/blog/7-risk-assessment-methods-to-streamline-risk-management/)
More specific details — CFA Institute. (2024). Measuring and Managing Market Risk. (https://www.cfainstitute.org/insights/professional-learning/refresher-readings/2024/measuring-managing-market-risk)

79: a) Kahneman, D., & Deaton, A. (2010). High income improves evaluation of life but not emotional well-being. Proceedings of the National Academy of Sciences, 107(38), 16489 — 16493. (https://doi.org/10.1073/pnas.1011492107)
b) *A breakdown of the study that disputes the one above. I find the study highly questionable; however, the way information is pushed to people, I don't doubt it will be touted as a counter-argument by some, so I wanted to address it. If you look at the main chart of the findings*

(Figure 2), at first glance, it looks like the data points were grouped to illustrate trends, but on further observation, you'll note that the "x" and "y" values mean that this isn't the case — each dot can only exist where it does. If this chart were accurate, it would mean that all humanity exists in five "tiers" of happiness, with nobody in between. Looking deeper than the chart of findings, it also bears mentioning that this study is at odds with a large body of psychological work examining depression rates in lower socio-economic communities, as well as the observations of many philosophies, including Stoicism, Buddhism, epicureanism, minimalism, and (in a broad sense) utilitarianism. If this study were accurate, then there would be no cap on happiness, and the best medication for clinical depression would be money. According to the study's results, if you continue the upward trend of happiness to even higher income levels, almost every multi-millionaire would live in a constant state of ecstasy. Beyond that, it implies that a $50k raise would improve happiness more for a person who already makes $150k each year than it would for a person who only makes $50k each year. The findings don't make sense when examined critically. This is why I say that this study reads more like propaganda. The findings don't make sense when examined critically. It's a good reminder that information — even studies — must be examined, not simply taken at face value. — Matthew A. Killingsworth, Daniel Kahneman, and Barbara Mellers (2022). Income and emotional well-being: A conflict resolved? *Proceedings of the National Academy of Sciences*, 120(12), e2300426120. (https://www.pnas.org/doi/10.1073/pnas.2208661120)

80: *Entry sanitation pay* — Zippia. (n.d.). Sanitation Worker Salary. (https://www.zippia.com/salaries/sanitation-worker/)
Entry postal services pay — ZipRecruiter. (n.d.). Entry-Level Postal Worker Salary. (https://www.ziprecruiter.com/Salaries/Entry-Level-Postal-Worker-Salary)
Entry DMV clerk pay — Zippia. (n.d.). Motor Vehicle Clerk Jobs. (https://www.zippia.com/motor-vehicle-clerk-jobs/)

81: *Teacher salaries* — Salary.com. (n.d.). Public School Teacher Salary. (https://www.salary.com/research/salary/benchmark/public-school-teacher-salary)

82: USAFacts. (2024). How much does the US spend on the military? (https://usafacts.org/articles/how-much-does-the-us-spend-on-the-military/)
Direct link to the full budget overview — U.S. Department of Defense. (2023). Fiscal Year 2024 Budget Request Overview Book. (https://comptroller.defense.gov/Portals/45/Documents/defbudget/FY2024/FY2024_Budget_Request_Overview_Book.pdf)

83: Global Firepower (2024). Defense Budget by Country (2024). (https://www.globalfirepower.com/defense-spending-budget.php)

84: *Overview* — Students of History. (n.d.). The Decline of the Roman Republic. (https://www.studentsofhistory.com/the-decline-of-the-roman-republic)
More in-depth and scholarly article discussing corruption and attempts to address it— Arena, V. (2017). Fighting Corruption: Political Thought and Practice in the Late Roman Republic. In *Anti-corruption in History: From Antiquity to the Modern Era*. Oxford University Press. (https://academic.oup.com/book/25798/chapter-abstract/193391684?redirectedFrom=fulltext&login=false)

85: *Throughout history, when you see people going on strike or protesting unfair pay, those people tend to be living and working in poor conditions. If they could get a better job, they would — but when better jobs aren't available or your lack of resources makes it hard to survive, much less get an education... your options are very limited. This is something that many employers have counted on to maximize their profits. A quick search for "labor exploitation" or "historic labor strikes" will give you several months of reading material to back up this point.*

86: Godlewski, N. (n.d.). Small Business Revenue Statistics. Fundera. Retrieved January 22, 2025, from (https://www.fundera.com/resources/small-business-revenue-statistics)

87: PayScale. (n.d.). Small Business Owner Salary. (https://www.payscale.com/research/US/Job=Small_Business_Owner/Salary)

Acknowledgements

I want to thank several people without whom this book would have taken months or years longer to complete — if I ever finished it at all.

Danielle Butler, my early-stage editor and guide in this process — thank you for all of your expertise in the indie publishing world. I appreciate all the time you spent guiding the early drafts of my book and advising me as I stepped into the world of published works for the first time. Also, thank you for your impeccable taste in cats; yours are most excellent.

Michael Mau, my editor and formatter — thank you for your patience as I committed likely three dozen editing/formatting faux pas. I appreciate your aid in turning this from a relentless wall of text and thought to something much more user-friendly.

Andy Meaden of Meaden Creative, the talent behind the cover. Thank you for your willingness to work with my vagaries to bring them into concrete reality. A book is often judged by its cover, and I deeply appreciate you for bearing with me to create a design that encapsulates what this book is about.

Ariane Smith, my proofreader — thank you for your keen eye and insightful feedback. Beyond catching little issues leftover from all the editing, your recommendations on word choice and transitions helped the book to flow much more naturally, while preserving my voice.

Cait Cortelyou, thank you for your encouragement and patience as the writing of this book consumed so much of my time. I deeply appreciate your belief, your encouragement, and your direction throughout the writing process. Thank you for your expert and insightful commentary and proofreading as you reined in my constant tangents and kept my train of thought on the tracks.

www.ingramcontent.com/pod-product-compliance
Lightning Source LLC
Chambersburg PA
CBHW051621120626
46551CB00014B/1891